Ella Young,
Irish Mystic and Rebel

ELLA YOUNG, IRISH MYSTIC AND REBEL

From Literary Dublin to the American West

Rose Murphy

The Liffey Press

Published by
The Liffey Press
Ashbrook House, 10 Main Street,
Raheny, Dublin 5, Ireland
www.theliffeypress.com

© 2008 Rose Murphy

A catalogue record of this book is
available from the British Library.

ISBN 978-1-905785-31-5

Printed in Ireland by Colour Books

Contents

Acknowledgements

To good friends and supporters in Ella Young's California home, Oceano: Norm Hammond, Oceano's resident historian for all his encouragement and generous sharing of local lore; Jim Cain, for access to his insightful, first-hand interviews with Ella's friends; Peggy Weedon, present owner of Ella Young's cottage, for preserving Ella's spirit and loaning me many priceless photos; Gudrun Grell, for colorful memories about her friendship with Ella.

To Risa Aratyr, for her expert editing and also for her knowledge of Celtic mythology.

To my proofreader son, Tony Murphy, for his attention to seemingly small, but vital, details.

To my publisher, David Givens of The Liffey Press, for believing in Ella's story, and to his wife Darina for adding her support.

To my husband Larry for reading through various twists of Ella's life, assisting in my photo search and accepting all the hours I spent holed up in an attic office.

To my writing group:

Maureen, Janet, Todd,
Wayne, Mary, and Lisa

for all your suggestions,
encouragement and unfailing good humour

Introduction

There once was a woman who died with an evil heart. By night her spirit haunted a certain road and killed all those who ventured down it. So frightful was this spirit that no one would dare go out after dusk, not even on an urgent errand. At last, a priest with extraordinary spiritual powers engaged the woman's ghost in a wrestling match. The priest prevailed over the evil spirit, the people could walk the road without fear, and – as Ella Young told the tale – "there was nothing [left] in the morning but a lump of jelly".

Eerie tales such as this one, gathered by Ella Young (1867-1956) in the early twentieth century, were typical of the western Ireland narratives treasured by this Irish writer, storyteller, teacher, poet, mystic, rebel, immigrant and westward adventurer. Her own life story, which included guarding weapons under floorboards for Irish rebels in the 1920s and bringing her Celtic tales to California audiences, has never emerged from the shadows of more famous luminaries. Poet William Butler Yeats and playwright Lady Gregory, among others in a major Irish literary revival, are often credited with reviving Irish culture buried under centuries of British rule. Yet, Ella Young was one of the diggers who unearthed old legends and adapted them for new generations. Always lured westward – from Dublin to Ireland's West to America – she eventually settled in California, where she became known in the 1930s and '40s as an unofficial Irish artist-in-residence.

Perhaps unwittingly, as her life and career progressed, she assumed the persona of the Irish "shanachie", or the old Gaelic storyteller. In Ireland, the traditional shanachie, the weaver of stories around hearths and in pubs, was invariably male. Long before oral tales were put between book covers, and well before television replaced the storyteller, he was welcomed in the cottages of Western Ireland, where he held forth with accounts of ancient folklore, heroic tales and local social history. Through the centuries, it was the shanachie who kept alive an oral Irish culture for succeeding generations. Although he has largely disappeared from the wired, tech-savvy Ireland of today, some older people still remember storytellers from their childhoods, when a lengthy saga, told on consecutive evenings around a hearth on cold winter nights, would not conclude until springtime.

Ella Young – female, Protestant and urban – might seem a contradiction to the image of the wizened, male, Irish Catholic storyteller in a peasant village. She was at once the urban outsider in the West and the faithful recorder of its traditions and heritage. Ella adapted the old Celtic legends for new Irish generations of young people, although "adapt" does not accurately describe her work. Critics agreed that she held on to the spirit and flavour of ancient tales, even as she updated them. She became the female shanachie by bringing traditional West of Ireland stories first to Dublin audiences, and then across the Atlantic and on to California.

But long before Ella even thought about emigrating, she moved into Dublin's literary and mystical circles. She departed dramatically from the traditional role of an upper-class Protestant woman, who was expected to become just well-enough educated and cultivated to attract a suitable husband, create a gracious home, and preside over the teapot.

Instead, Ella threw herself into a movement that revived what was considered to be authentic Irish culture; she also played a substantial role in Ireland's struggle for independence. Like Ella, many other players of that movement were Protestant. Their families had lived in Ireland for centuries and considered themselves to be every bit as Irish as the traditional Catholic farmer. Their allegiance to Ireland became more important to them than old family ties to England. Because the Protestant Irish generally came from the upper classes, they tended to be better educated than most of the Catholic population and were therefore better able to articulate the cause of Irish self-governance and to promote the native Irish stories. Ella's Northern Irish roots came from Presbyterian ancestors, the Scots settlers who poured into Northern Ireland beginning in the seventeenth century, many placed on the land by the British in order to counter the more numerous Catholic natives.

Her Dublin contemporaries included such luminaries as W. B. Yeats, activist Maud Gonne, and playwright J.M. Synge, all of whom garnered far more space in books on the Irish Literary Renaissance than Ella did. Yet, she was certainly in the forefront of bringing authentic Irish tales and old Celtic myths onto the printed page. Perhaps this lack of recognition stems from the fact that Ella's published works on Celtic mythology were written largely for young people. While her storytelling events and college lectures addressed mainly adult audiences, and in a highly mesmerising and entertaining style, according to reports of Ella's day, these oral presentations could not be preserved and experienced again, as could the solid and lasting books in print.

Admittedly, Ella played a modest role in her impact on the public's consciousness of Ireland's native oral literature, but what follows is not a critical biography in the usual sense of the term. Rather, I have portrayed her as a fascinating, puzzling and noteworthy woman whose life story is worth telling simply to highlight a flamboyant and dramatic Irish personality whose place in twentieth century Irish culture and literature has been undervalued. Also, she placed a perceptive mirror, for twenty-first century readers, in front of key events in Ireland and provided an unusual insider's view of major artistic figures in two countries.

Ella definitely looked to Ireland's past for inspiration, as did many Dublin writers and artists who saw "the West" of Ireland as the sacred source of pure Celtic culture, a place of unspoiled simplicity that had retained its Irish identity despite British attempts to impose the coloniser's language and culture. On one occasion, when Ella arrived at a small western village, she waited for the expected "jaunting car" – a two-wheeled, horse-drawn, open cart conveying a few passengers on plank-like seats behind the driver – to take her to her lodgings at a local farmhouse. When no such vehicle arrived, she set off walking: "There is a strange delight in following an unknown road at dusk ... some adventures lie at the end of it.... The magic of the West held me, as it always did." Her fascination with westward locales eventually extended to New York and New England, where she soon experienced the American immigrant pull toward the next horizon, the exotic lure of the last stop at the edge of the continent: California.

Across America, and especially in California, large audiences, including homesick immigrants and first-generation Irishmen, gathered in auditoriums and lecture halls and libraries to hear Ella Young's tales from her western Irish adventures. As a lecturer at the University of California at Berkeley she drew in both academic and general listeners with lyrical tales of spirits in Irish hills and larger-than-life mythical heroes. She also discovered new artistic communities and friendships with California's cultural icons of the day: a picnic with poet Robinson Jeffers; a car trip to New Mexico with photographer Ansel Adams; conversations and Irish whiskey on a beach near San Luis Obispo with astrologer Gavin Arthur, grandson of the American president Chester A. Arthur.

Ella could not have imagined all those encounters while she was caught up in her own land's maelstrom of momentous historical events. During the War of Independence (1916-1921) and the Civil War that followed, she and her contemporaries in the Irish Literary Renaissance saw their artistry as a force in Ireland's battle, their stories and plays as essential weapons. By making Irish people aware of their proud heritage, the revivalists hoped to give their countrymen a sense of national pride that would move them to throw off British rule once and for all.

Ella herself knew, at least intellectually, that the Irish could not match England's superior military power, but she was convinced that Ireland could prevail by encouraging nationhood:

> It is true that we have no hope of an armed thrust at the might of England, but we can tear to pieces the calumnies with which she strives to hide her exploitation. We can revive our ancient culture and our language. The sagas and hero-tales even now are spreading amongst us as oil spreads upon water, iridescent and inescapable.

Even as she admitted there was "no hope" in battling the coloniser, she became an ardent supporter of the independence movement. In 1914 she engaged in gunrunning for the rebels (the Irish Volunteers, forerunners of the Irish Republican Army), and later endured police searches in her Dublin home, where weapons for the rebels were hidden. She always regarded this rebel activity as completely harmonious with her study of spirits, Irish myths, and warrior tales; she saw what seemed an obvious link between the stories of ancient heroes and a national need for heroes in the twentieth century. Poet Padraic Colum once said of Ella's storytelling, "When she retells something from myth or folklore, she is not merely relating an interesting legend: she is telling part of a sacred history."

The personality of this passionate advocate for Ireland's "sacred history" was one of contrasts. The same woman who engaged in gunrunning for the rebels also wrote airy books of Celtic literature and dabbled in the occult with other Dublin mystics. She heard fairy music, which she described as "sweeter than singing voices ... parts of an orchestra", yet her nationalist sympathies led to the inclusion of her name on a British "black list" of activist nationalists. As for her probable lesbianism, that factor is irrelevant to my story of the unknown Irish storyteller pushing westward. Nor is it my intention to look at her life through a contrived, lesbian-feminist lens.

It is true that Ella would not have called herself a feminist; yet, her life choices all pointed toward an independent woman who set her own course. Alone, as she approached her 58th birthday in 1925, she found the courage to board a ship and cross the Atlantic to an America she knew only the from gold-in-the-street descriptions of Catholic Irish immigrants. Among immigrant women of all ethnic groups, Irish women held the distinction of most often coming to America alone or with sisters or friends, rather than with husbands, fathers or other presumably protective family males.

From our modern perspective, we can only guess at the determination it took to leave behind everything familiar and venture into an unknown land. Granted, Ella was not among the mostly impoverished women enticed to America by its promise of riches, women who left Ireland in droves in the post-famine years. Yet the Protestant, upper-class Ella shared with some Catholic sister immigrants a willingness to look westward and to move beyond the more familiar and Irish-populated East Coast into America's West.

It is also worth pointing out that while Yeats and others of the Irish Revival movement lectured around the United States, she was virtually alone among her Dublin contemporaries in emigrating to America. Ella's friend, the poet Padraic Colum, did settle in New England, but most artists of the Irish Literary Revival preferred to live and work in the country they wrote about.

While Ella felt fully rooted in California and became a United States citizen, her life in America was devoted to bringing the culture of Ireland into American consciousness and promoting an awareness of her native land's struggle to become fully free and united. Today, her books of stories and poetry sit largely unnoticed on library shelves despite her many contributions to an understanding of Ireland's rich culture and her well-known status on the California lecture circuit from the 1920s through to the 1950s. She always spoke of Ireland as though she herself had lived in ancient times, as though no one would ever dispute her reports of conversations with trees and of her reincarnated lives.

It is tempting to imagine that Ella's career in storytelling was carefully choreographed – à la Hollywood – to project a colourful and slightly wacky façade, one that sold an abundance of lecture tickets. But, after pouring through her writings, records of friends and interviews with the few alive who knew her, I concluded that Ella was completely open and sincere about all her mystical beliefs, about the other world of spirits that existed along with our more earthbound realm.

Ella Young would have appreciated, I think, that I have kept my focus on stories, concentrating on those that illustrate her devotion to authentic Irish culture and her enthusiasm for America's West. From her autobiography, *Flowering Dusk: Things Remembered Accurately and Inaccurately,* come accounts of Irish lore, Dublin's artistic giants, Ireland's struggle for independence, and her immigrant experiences in California. Perhaps Ella embellished or embroidered a few events from her autobiography; to her, the story itself was all-important, and some flourishes only served to celebrate the spirit of Gaelic storytelling.

Beyond *Flowering Dusk*, I found treasure troves of letters, poems, pamphlets and personal journals in sites as diverse as Trinity College in Dublin; the University of California at Los Angeles; Bancroft Library at the University of California at Berkeley (where she taught for seven years); and a tiny, eclectic, and jewel-filled library (still with a card file system!) in the Irish Cultural Center in San Francisco. From Ella's own words and the words of those who knew her, a picture emerges of a writer and mystic who became a fervent rebel, and then emigrant.

Although the book is loosely chronological, the chapters are arranged according to important themes in Ella's life. The story moves from her birth in Northern Ireland to early childhood signs of a mystical nature, to the magical stories she collected in the West of Ireland, to her years in Dublin and associations with its Irish Revival enthusiasts. The story then embraces her emigration to New York and her move to California, her exploration of California's spirits and spirituality, her friendships with American icons of the 1920s and her legacy of published works on Celtic culture.

Ella did not come to embrace native Irish lore and storytelling early in life. Her roots lay in a traditional, Presbyterian, upper middle class lifestyle of some privilege, although her childhood and early adulthood offer some clues into her transformation.

Chapter 1

From Childhood Ghosts to Dublin Mystics

"Somewhere there must be folk who think as I do."

Long before she explored California's spirits, Ella met her own personal ghost in her family's Portarlington home, in a house built by a French count. She was probably eleven or twelve years old when this spirit (not the French count!) suddenly appeared one night at the foot of her bed. Other family members had noticed some wispy, mysterious movements around the house; sister Elizabeth had seen "a tall figure go whitely by in the dusk", and their mother had been awakened by strange noises.

This ghost appeared definitively in Ella's room on several occasions, a gentle spirit who stood at the foot of her bed and sometimes seemed poised to speak, but then simply sighed. Ella was sure that the ghost was womanly. Upon leaving, "she moved softly from the room: as she went, her silken skirts made a sound around her". After several nights, Ella had lost all fear *of this apparition and had, in fact, become quite comfortable with the presence. Ella neither cowered under the covers nor called for her mother. On one occasion, she called out to the ghost, invoking the symbols of her Presbyterian faith: "In the name of the Trinity, Father, Son, and Holy Ghost, speak! I am not afraid to listen." But the ghost merely sighed again and soon departed.*

Ella felt that the ghost was heavy-hearted, saddened by some weighty matter. She imagined the misty woman walking the grounds outside of the house, perhaps slipping into the spooky meadows that bordered the Barrow River below the Young estate.

As an adult, Ella would find it quite natural to accept that the dead returned to roam among the living. She later mused about that early ghost: "Do those who have said farewell to life and put off the burden of the flesh, sigh at times and remember?" It is tempting to surmise, although impossible to know, that the apparition represented a sign that Ella would one day immerse herself in the independence struggle of Ireland, often personified by a symbol of the old woman transformed into a beautiful woman, Cathleen Ni Houlihan, who purportedly called a nation to save her and sacrifice themselves for her.

Ella Young was born in Northern Ireland, County Antrim, in the townland of Fenagh in the Presbyterian parish of Ahogill, to James Bristow Young and Matilda Ann Russell Young on December 25, or December 26, 1867, depending on the source. She was probably the oldest of six siblings, although, again, records and Ella's rambling autobiography provide varying information. Throughout her life, she referred most consistently to four sisters

– Jennie, Maude, Elizabeth and Mary – and briefly to a brother, Morogh.

Ella always cherished her Northern Ireland roots in a lush country she remembered as rounded hills and wet bogs, a land purple with heather, and dense wooded glens looking down over the water where a salty sea tang blew in from the North Channel. She seemed early on to have breathed in an instinctive appreciation for this landscape and the native Irish who lived there: "I have always believed that the countryside where one is born leaves its mark on a person. . . . My father's people and my mother's folk have called the land their own for more than three centuries."

Throughout her life, Ella always identified with the city of Dublin, but when she was three years old, her family first moved from Northern Ireland to Limerick, near the Shannon River. Ella remembered Limerick as a "huddlement of red brick" houses and a place "sunk in Catholicism and Episcopalian orthodoxy", a dominance that no doubt required some adjustment for the Young family from Northern Ireland's Presbyterian enclave. Limerick had always had a reputation for being a staunch Catholic nationalist town, going back to seventeenth century sieges of the city by the British.

The Youngs could accurately be described as upper middle class, but without the wealth and the rank of some members of the ruling Church of Ireland Ascendancy, whose grand estates swept wide swaths of the Irish landscape. The Ireland of Ella's childhood was a land mostly recovered from the ravages of the 1846–47 famine, although a slightly better quality of life for the native Irish was largely due to the continuing emigration of people looking for opportunity in America, thus easing the pressures of population at home. The grip of the Protestant Ascendancy, the ruling class, was slowly loosening, as the Catholic nationalist movement grew stronger. Fading irreversibly were the days when Anglo aristocrats reigned completely over the native Irishmen who often lived in wretched quarters down the hill from the "Big House", and these grand Protestant homes must have appeared quite majestic from the view of a peasant family in a tiny cottage below. At the same time, use of the Irish language was declining dramatically as British control automatically defined English as the essential language of survival in schools, offices and the endless transactions of daily life.

As a child, Ella did not question the order of things: Protestants ran most businesses and government and held most of the land, while Catholics generally tilled meagre fields and worked in settings like the Young household. In her recollections, Ella dropped hints about the family's modest affluence: the walled garden and meadows, the servant putting her to bed, the mother "who took no interest in the kitchen" beyond listening to the cook's complaints.

Later, probably as a teenager, Ella lived in Portarlington, near the famous Bog of Allen and on the Barrow River, south and west of Dublin. The town had first been settled by French Huguenots in the seventeenth century, refugees fleeing France's persecution of Protestants. When Ella and her family went on shopping excursions from the ghost-haunted home formerly of the French count, they noted the many storefronts, family names and churches with the imprint of French influence. Ella sought out the lonely, nearby Bog of Allen, a vast stretch of peat bog enlivened by eclectic arrays of wildflowers, where "there is a spot that must be the Fountain of Youth, for when I stand there, I feel a great joy surging through me ... I go there when I can, always alone".

Both in Limerick and Portarlington, Ella's life was a pleasant experience that signified some affluence – rowing boats, riding horses and, above all, reading. Books were treasured; her mother's favourite poet was the American Henry Wadsworth Longfellow, and Ella remembered hearing his poems read to her "from a big book, gorgeous in tooled leather and gilt edges". At an early age, "almost as soon as I could read with ease", Ella read Shakespeare in adult editions, noting that "my father would not allow Lamb's Tales From Shakespeare [children's versions]". Her later passion for literature sprang from the encouragement of both mother and father whose reading interests obviously extended well beyond the Bible and Presbyterian tracts.

Ella's artistic leanings were further bolstered by the makeshift theatre she and sister Jennie put together in a room provided by their mother. They put on impromptu plays, composing lines as they went along, never bothered by a lack of audience. "High Tragedy was our forte", according to Ella; they staged maudlin tragedies in which the chief characters inevitably collapsed in death as the curtain fell. "We never thought about how ridiculous we looked." Ridiculous or not, her thespian adventures planted the seeds of a later passion for dramatic tales.

Her formal education, in her view, did not evoke positive memories: "I made myself obnoxious at school and stood high in no one's estimation." Perhaps her early mystical bent set her apart from school friends and the obligatory sewing class. She remembered one special epiphany, of running across a field to her father, when:

> ... suddenly I stumbled and nearly fell. At the same time, I was aware of a strange light of radiance that was gathering, not so much in the outer air as in my mind and being. Not with my *eyes*, I saw one of the *others* [my italics]. "Who are you?" I asked, and the reply came. Since that day I have spoken with *them*.

In her memoirs, Ella did not share the reply from "them", but nevertheless felt that she had definitely communicated with the spirit.

There were also signs that Ella was not enthralled with the obligatory Bible and Catechism readings in her home. So devout was the family that her father often had services and sermons performed at home by a minister. But on other Sundays, Ella endured the ritual "in the solemn ugly Presbyterian Church". She came to dread Sundays not only for those tedious church hours, but also because the weekday childhood pleasures were banished: "no toys, no picture books, no hide-and-seek in the garden". In the family pew, she and her sister Jennie passed the time during ponderous sermons by working off the red plush buttons from the seat cushions, patiently loosening them a little more each Sunday and competing over who could unpluck the treasure first. "My mother wondered why the cushions had to have buttons sewn on so frequently."

As she grew older, Ella struggled mightily to repent for the sinfulness that apparently, from dire warnings constantly intoned by the minister, permeated her being. She began to fear that she "might die in the night and drop into Hell! Before I went to sleep, I [knew] I must repent. I would kneel by my bed trying to squeeze out a tear." Still, the nighttime fear of Hell and the hold of conventional religion on Ella were tenuous, even when surrounded by its strictures. She wondered if she could endure Hell, since that seemed to be the direction she was heading; one day she slipped into the empty drawing room, closed the door and said aloud: "God, I hate you! I wish the devil had won when he fought against you." After exhausting all efforts to "praise God", whatever that meant, she prepared for the worst. "I knew it meant going to Hell. I would have to stand it. Millions and millions of people managed to do it. I had an idea that I might like some of these people – I knew I would not like the people who went to Heaven."

In her teens and early adulthood, she continued this drift from the Church, began writing, and lost some of her enthusiasm for

Portarlington, longing for more excitement than was available in Ireland's midlands: "Somewhere there must be folk who think as I do, people who would greet me as a comrade." Ironically, Ella would one day seek out the quiet of small villages and farms, rather than the urban excitement of Dublin, as she gathered lore from the West of Ireland. She was delighted when the family moved to Dublin in the 1890s, where they settled in the Rathmines district, south of the city centre. Still, she had some complaints about the new Young home: "The house is small and mean-looking: it has many rooms but not a single spacious one. Crowding on either side of it are similar houses – their presence heightens the general effect of comfortless gentility." Ella referred to the brick row houses of Rathmines' Grosvenor Square where a certain Victorian respectability prevailed, even though the family's walls adjoined neighbouring homes.

When Ella took the nearby tram into Dublin proper, she travelled into a city full of raucous noise, where streetcars rumbled by on steel tracks, bells clanging. Horse carriage wheels clicked along cobblestones, and still-novel motor cars sputtered through town, horns honking to call attention to a marvellous gas-powered invention. Street sellers hawked their wares, everything from violets to oranges to newspapers, while organ grinders with their hurdy-gurdy tunes competed with balladeers who sang on street corners for a few pence.

Ella hoped that "Dublin [had] theatres and concert halls". Such cultural venues were far removed from another side of the city: the vast majority of the Catholic populace lived in wretched slums where large families crammed into tiny flats and diseases raged through the squalid neighbourhoods. Family sizes of seven, eight, nine children might have been even larger, were it not for the fact that many babies did not survive infancy. Those who did survive grew up barefoot in alleyways and could scarcely write their

names. Ella would one day teach the old Celtic tales to the barefoot children of the alleyways.

In 1893 Ella began study at Dublin's Royal University; this
lover of all things magical studied economics and law, but as her
friend and mentor George Russell (AE) once noted, "No one would
have suspected it". After graduation, she became a schoolteacher,
the accepted profession for young Protestant women.

At the turn of the twentieth century, she was in her early thirties, and perhaps her family saw her headed for a spinster's life.
Did her parents arrange for Ella to receive suitors in the parlour in
Rathmines, pleasant young men with good prospects? It is impossible to know if or when she realised her probable lesbianism, nor
to know if her parents were aware of her sexual orientation. Perhaps the issue never came up; perhaps Ella simply decided, as
time went on, that she wanted to explore the world of ideas and
learning, rather than embroidery and tea rituals. Certainly, a lesbian lifestyle would have been unacceptable in a conservative, still
Victorian, urban Irish society.

A clue to her sexual orientation occurred once during the hated
Sunday church obligations of her childhood, a day when the tedium was broken. In the midst of a droning hymn, she caught
sight of a beautiful little girl "with brown-gold hair curled on either side of a pale face.... She was like the first sunlight on a day of
Winter. The ice in my heart broke up. All my ideas about God and
the Universe tumbled to destruction.... I was no longer a prisoner
in a pew.... So for the first time I saw Brysanthe. She was seven
years old. I was nine." In her memoirs, Ella showered this ecstatic
praise on a childhood friend, and obviously it became a significant
life memory. Long after Ella had died, an article in the California
lesbian periodical of Elsa Gidlow referred to this event and noted:

"This [was] only the first of her praise of the beauty of women – she who refused to praise God."[1]

Ella never chose to write overtly about her sexual preferences; early in her Dublin adventures, she focused more on a spiritual search, and she was drawn to intellectuals and artists who were also searching and experimenting. Ella travelled far from the staid Presbyterian family pew through her introduction to the Theosophical society. Members of this mystical society met regularly in Dublin, practicing rituals that combined spiritual teachings of East and West. Theosophy, literally "knowledge of the divine", gained popularity among European intellectuals through the teachings of a Russian noblewoman, Madame Blavatsky, who promoted a blend of Christian compassion, occult practice and belief in reincarnation. In her first Theosophical meetings, Ella was dazzled by speakers who talked of "dream-consciousness, voyages in the astral, cycles of reincarnation."

Many Theosophists were also members of the Irish Literary Revival, the artists who were putting old Irish tales into print, staging them, and also learning the Irish language. Soon, Celtic literature became Ella's religion, as she drew inspiration from these new Dublin colleagues. She began her forays into the West of Ireland, collecting its stories and lore, and launched into a life's work that would carry her ever westward.

---

[1] From a letter to this prominent lesbian writer, who quoted it in her publication *Women Spirit* (Winter 1976), a connection that suggested Ella Young's own lesbianism.

Chapter 2

Spirits and Caves
in the West of Ireland

"The magic of the west held me."

One day, in Ireland's remote Connemara region, on a gnarled finger of rugged land crooking westward from Galway town, Ella decided to be bold and try out a few simple Gaelic sentences with a bearded man sitting on a wall who "looked like a Greek in the age of Pericles". To her delight, she was understood: "My Gaelic did not smack too much of school books and Dublin." The fellow, Padraic Greene by name, immediately became a friend; he had a sailing boat, and Ella persuaded him to arrange an outing that included her travelling companions.

The group set out across Galway Bay for Inis Mor, the largest of the three Aran Islands. Here, hardy residents tended sheep on rocky snippets of land and snagged a few fish by braving the waters of the Atlantic in flimsy boats called "currachs". On the day of Ella's outing, however, massive waves buffeted Padraic's *sailing boat and sent all its occupants back to shore, into a quiet green inlet where other boats had taken shelter. Among the men sitting in boats near his own, waiting for placid waters, Padraic recognised a renowned scholar and shanachie, a Gaelic storyteller.*

Ella's group begged for a story from him, so they all gathered into one boat: Ella, her friends, Padraic and the local fishermen. The shanachie stood among them, his listeners lined up on either side. In the tradition of Gaelic storytellers, they were allowed to sit because his story was prose. Had it been poetry, considered a nobler form of literature, the audience would have been obliged to stand, posing a somewhat tricky manoeuvre in a boat.

Ella found it a "long and splendid story ... [even though I] could not follow it very well". Padraic gushed over it extravagantly: "What a jewel of a story! Wasn't that hero the champion of the world!" Ella felt somewhat chastened by Padraic's superior grasp of the tale, although it turned out that he had understood very little of it. He later explained to Ella: "It's the old, old Irish out of the old times, and this man had the words of it from his father, and he from his father again, and back and back, till an eagle couldn't remember it – or the oldest tree. He has the very words. He didn't change them."

Padraic had praised the story because of the shanachie's status in the community, but also because – in some intuitive connection with his culture – Padraic had picked up at least the thread of the tale: a warrior who had taken the shape of a bird and had gone to the rescue of a fellow warrior carried over the sea by a hostile king. Ella learned that the storyteller had come from a long line of shanachies. She surmised: "His ancestors may have told this story to pleasure the kings of Connaught."

To the West of Ireland folk whom Ella met during her travels in the early 1900s, tales once told to the "kings of Connaught" meant little in their daily lives. But tales told to them by the local shanachie meant everything. It was he who served as the community's link to what seemed a glorious, golden past filled with heroes who provided a sense of pride and heritage for a colonised people. He also told stories of eerie premonitions and prophecies about death, as did the "red-bearded, blue-eyed shanachie from Devenish Island [off the coast of County Kerry]" whom Ella met on one of her ramblings. Ella asked him to relate the strangest happening on his island. "The queerest happening," he told her, "was the time the boat came in from nowhere."

He told of the day that he was alone in the house and thinking of his uncle who was perhaps on his deathbed, "for a heavy sickness had gripped him". The shanachie saw an unfamiliar boat coming into the cove, filled with strangers save for one man: his uncle. The man tilling the boat urged the shanachie to join them, for "we have come a long way for you". But the uncle intervened and warned his nephew not to get on board. "Don't put your foot on the boat ... or you'll never put foot on the Island again. And bid us begone now, and turn your face to your own house door." The shanachie did as his uncle directed and turned homeward as the boat pulled away without him. "I had a fear on me. I sat in the sun and recited the Rosary...." Later, he learned that his uncle was dead.

Ella Young, the proper, Protestant, urban woman, came to appreciate such tales from the West of Ireland's native Catholics and fell under the mesmerising spell of their stories. She became the unlikely female shanachie who took Ireland's story from little westerly communities into all of Ireland and on to the West Coast of America. Nevertheless, the better-known Lady Gregory earned greater fame for unearthing Irish lore than did Ella.

Lady Gregory was co-founder of a national Irish theatre, a playwright and a Protestant landowner in County Clare. She spent hours in mean little cottages near her home, gathering folklore from her neighbours. Ella also collected such tales at hearthsides, but it was Lady Gregory who became famous for her ability to capture local colour, ultimately publishing stories that vividly illuminated the Irish peasant life and customs of the West. Despite her aristocratic upbringing, Lady Gregory was an ardent nationalist who saw that the days of Anglo-Irish landowners were dwindling in the face of uprisings by tenant farmers.

The younger Ella shared that view even as she was still forming her own nationalist stance. By the turn of the century, when she was in her early thirties, Ella was influenced by the writings of the great cultural historian, Standish O'Grady, and had made her first trip into the West of Ireland with his wife, Margaret. Standish believed that the Anglo-Irish estate owners and landlords had much to gain from joining in the native Irish cause. As Ella phrased Standish's ideas:

> If they [landowners] were made aware of what a proud and ancient culture they could claim as Irishmen – if they realised that they must throw in their fortunes with their countrymen or lose both lands and authority, they would save themselves: they would head the "New Ireland Movement" rather than lag behind and be destroyed by it.

While Lady Gregory actually lived among the people whose lives she recorded, the urban Ella relied on trains to carry her westward. For her first journey, Ella was given a free ticket by Margaret O'Grady, which had been intended for her husband Standish, who could not make the trip. Ella was expected to fill in for Standish and earn her fare by writing accounts of scenery and people for a railway company article. Happily, she wrote glowing prose about all she saw and experienced. When the railway company discovered that the resulting article did not come from Standish, however, Ella correctly predicted that she would never receive another free ticket. Still, she managed to fund later trips on her own. In her memoirs, Ella's early impressions of Ireland's western region bordered on the ecstatic:

> My first glimpse of the West! My first experience of an enchantment that has held me all my life. Those little lakes with the sedges, those unplowable bogs, those windblown trees, those reaches of sand where the waves lap and make a song for the seabirds – lonely, untrodden reaches by the sea . . . the stone-walled cottages so securely thatched; the generous fireplace . . . the raftered ceiling; the stories by the smouldering turf-sods; the dawns, the sunsets, the unbelievable beauty!

Ella was just as lyrical in describing the people who invited her into their homes to tell their stories. Her description of a family who had once given her shelter had something of a fairy-tale quality:

> The man of the house, the golden-haired daughter, the son who had handled the reins on so many journeys across bog and stone-land, and the woman of the house. In Gaelic Ireland, the woman is always the head of the house.... This woman ... gracious, kindly featured, nimble-witted.

In truth, "the woman of the house" was generally too haggard to be "gracious" and might well be worn out by thirty, consigned to almost yearly childbearing. If she seemed to be the head of house, that role often sprang from necessity while her husband lifted pints at the local pub. This scenario raises uncomfortable images of a national Irish stereotype, but it proved true enough among Irish families and cannot be disregarded as a reality for many women. Some rural women did manage to carve out a bit of economic independence through cottage crafts or raising chickens. Some used the funds to ship the "golden-haired daughter" off to America for a presumably better future than that of wife to a neighbouring farmer on a barren piece of land.

Ella's primary interest was literary, not sociological, and she was searching for stories and lore not generally available in eastern Ireland. "The West" usually refers to the region west of the River Shannon, most of it within the ancient Irish province of Connaught. It remained largely Irish-speaking long after the east, north and south had been overpowered by the English language. Those latter areas were more influenced by Norman, Scottish and English settlers over the centuries, while the West retained its native Irish language and social customs. Because the most western regions of Ireland, in Connaught, were filled with mountains and bogs and offered little decent farmland, conquerors generally tended to ignore the place in their quest to control Ireland. Oliver Cromwell, certainly the most feared of English invaders, removed Irish landowners with the command: either accept English rule or go "to Hell or to Connaught", equating the province with the worst kind of banishment.

In contrast to Cromwell, Ella and her Dublin associates found the area endlessly appealing and rich with symbols of authentic Irish culture. Poet William Butler Yeats believed that many natives of the West lived lives that had never been expressed in literature. He advised another writer of the Irish Literary Renaissance, John Millington Synge, to explore the westernmost reaches of Ireland, where Irish peasant stories were presumably waiting to be discovered. Synge did, in fact, live for periods of time on Inis Meáin, the middle Aran Island, and he became regarded as one of the early recorders of Irish culture. He published his findings together with his own photographs in a book called *The Aran Islands*, which is an account of the islands' people and stories.

Even the mighty James Joyce, who eschewed a movement that looked to the past and instead pursued a modernist, international stream of literature, recognised the power of the West. In his classic story "The Dead," the character named Gabriel – who bears some resemblance to Joyce himself – is chided by the ardent nationalist, Miss Ivors, for spending his vacations on the Continent, rather than in Western Ireland, a locale more fitting for good, patriotic Irishmen. For both patriots and Literary Renaissance devotees, the idea of "the West" carried an aura of discovery, authenticity, revival and new beginnings.

Inspired by this movement, Ella continued to gather her stories from the West, including what might be called folk legends about strange happenings with strong tinges of magic. Many Irish peasants were comfortable with supernatural, unexplainable events, finding nothing unusual, for example, about accounts of successful curses that revenged wrongdoings. Quite matter-of-factly, Ella was told about the tavern keeper who accused a servant boy of stealing five pounds from the till, an act considered a capital offence. The boy was hanged, but the money was later found. As Ella recalled the story, the distraught mother placed a curse on the tavern owner, swearing that the man "would lose house, land and gear, die ragged and poverty-stricken in a ditch". Indeed, his cattle died, his wealth melted away and, as the mother predicted, he died by the roadside in a ditch.

Ella learned that an ancient ritual governed the act of cursing. The person who invokes the curse must be deeply injured and deprived of justice. Such a person must bring witnesses, declare the accusation and cite the accused, who may or may not be present. The wronged person kneels with both knees bared on the earth and invokes earth, air, fire, water and the Supreme Lord. The curse, which is always quite definite, is declared aloud. Did the endurance of tales of curses, of powerful people getting their comeuppance, stem from a colonised and downtrodden people's desire to imagine some control, however illusory, over their lives? Ella undoubtedly saw that connection as she absorbed the stories, and she developed an understanding of how the native culture, language and prestige were being overrun by the coloniser.

Ella came to see how certain tales affected people's daily lives. Local folk near the town of Cong north of Galway told her that deep inside a nearby cave, known as the Cave of the Red Steeds, lay treasures, mounds of golden goblets and shields of finest bronze. Yet anyone who ventured inside to claim the treasures either disappeared or left hurriedly, as if fleeing some terrible vision. Once, a piper entered. The locals heard his music grow fainter and fainter, and the poor fellow was never seen nor his piping heard again. Despite the rumours of those glittering stockpiles, no one would go near enough even to peek inside. Furthermore, terrified villagers and farmers occasionally saw wild red steeds emerge from the cave's mouth; thus its name. Sometimes water gushed out in a torrent, so people surmised that an underground river flowed within.

One person, who managed to escape before the cave could claim him, told of finding the river and on the brink of it "a woman who was rinsing blood-stained warrior gear in the waters". When Ella heard about the woman by this underground river, she grew excited: "I could name that River, and name the woman too. It is the River that separates the world of the living from the world of the dead: and the Woman is ... Macha." In Celtic mythology, Macha, a mother goddess and an aggressive warrior, was said to have killed her own brother in order to become queen of Ireland, thus the "bloodstained warrior gear". When Ella referred to the goddess Macha as the woman "rinsing blood-stained warrior gear", she was reaching into her vast store of knowledge about

Celtic mythology, a study that she had begun in Dublin and a subject for several of her books for young people.

Ella immediately wanted to explore the cave, although she knew her hosts would never accompany her. "No one will go in with you," said the woman of the house. "It is a terrible thing to think of you going in by yourself." Ella recalled her response: "I assured her that I was used to caves. I had crawled into caves. In caves I had sat solitary. I had gone by boat into caves where the sea groaned and snorted like a wounded beast." In a compromise, the family agreed to accompany Ella to the cave's entrance but would wait for her outside. They gave her three wax candles "which had been lit on Saint Brighid's Feast, and specially blest for an emergency". They also pressed upon her "a ball of twine to unwind", which she could unravel as she went deeper inside and then use to guide her back out of the cave when she was finished.

News of Ella's foolhardy plan quickly spread in the community, and a sizable crowd watched as she squirmed inside the opening of the Cave of the Red Steeds and found herself in a lofty chamber. From there, she could see a series of caves descending ever lower, one after another. Ella was entranced by the dark depths and the palpable spiritual silence, although she found no river and no gold treasures. Still, she had the sense that "a Fountain of Youth jets upward in it [the cave] from the Heart of the Earth...." Ella wanted to prolong her stay, sure that in the divine silence she "might attain to a state of spiritual perception in which Time, Space and Fate shriveled into nothingness". But she knew that the crowd gathered outside was anxiously waiting for her, frightened by the prospect that she might become one of the disappeared. When she emerged alive and triumphant, the onlookers clamoured for news of the treasure. Learning that none existed, they went away disillusioned and disappointed, back to their grim cottages.

The family that had reluctantly accompanied her to the Cave of the Red Steeds also showed Ella a tall standing stone which they believed marked the burial site of Lugh, the sun god. Ella knew his story, calling him the "Master of Every Craft", a reference to Lugh's many gifts and skills. He could appear under various disguises while waging battle, thus outwitting his opponents, a talent that gave him special standing among the gods. Throughout her life, Ella celebrated *Lughnasa*, the Celtic festival named for this god, which is observed on the first day of August in honour of the harvest.

Not far from Lugh's stone, Ella felt the presence of the goddess Dana. She was the mother of a whole brood of gods collectively known as the "People of the Goddess Danu", all powerful and colourful figures in Irish lore. On this rocky land, Ella imagined them vividly, moving "in a desert of stone ... in haunted knolls. White horses, a flaunt of many-coloured mantles, strange head-dresses they had. It was good for a man to veil his eyes as they passed." Always, Ella had the ability to look at a seemingly lifeless landscape, especially in the sparest, most rugged of places, and fill it with gods, colour and motion.

Although she loved all the tales of gods and folk heroes, Ella's sense of another world also introduced her to fairies, those little people who traditionally cavorted in Irish meadows and mountains, and who could bring good luck or ill fortune. Over centuries, the most famous symbol of these wispy creatures has been the mounds of earth left conspicuously uncultivated in fields by farmers who were reluctant to disturb the domains, or "rings", where the fairies congregated. Even in today's ultra-modern Ireland of high-tech firms and cell phones, one can still see these mounds rising out of the farming landscape. Many modern Irishmen still show ambivalence about the little people, as shown in the response of the Galway woman who was asked by an American anthropologist if she believed in fairies: "No, but they're there anyway."

Ella believed in the fairies as much as did the farmers carefully ploughing around their mounds. Furthermore, she was convinced that the creatures also lurked in mountains, meadows and trees. She knew they existed because she had heard their music. Ella described in great detail how "the power to hear [their music]" came to her in her early thirties when she was visiting Achill Island, a remote, wind-swept peninsula thrusting out of County Mayo's coastline. At first, she heard nothing, even as friends would stop in their tracks, cock their ears, and inquire of her: "Did you hear that?" Slowly, she began to be aware of what Gaelic speakers called *Ceol Sidhe*, or "music of the faery hills", the sounds first coming as suggestions of music, as mere snatches of voices, and maybe an occasional flute note.

Over the years, her power developed, until she heard music that was "orchestral and of amazing richness and complexity". At times, the separate parts of it did not seem to be totally harmonious; Ella noted "voices that wrangle and seem to shout aimlessly; clamorous, clangourous voices that do not repeat a rhythm on one note, yet the turmoil they make resolves itself into harmony with the whole". Her language grew ever more rhapsodic as she described the instrumental side of the music: "This faerie music has in it the sound of every instrument used in a great orchestra, and the sounds of many, many instruments that no orchestra possesses." Ella recounted all these details with passionate conviction; fairies not only existed, but to her, they formed grand symphonic orchestras. So entranced was Ella with this extravaganza of fairy music that for several nights she kept journal entries in which she reported that the sounds seemed to suggest "a procession of musicians [passing] close ... [with] bagpipes and cymbals and tinkling instruments ... a music as of stricken anvils, as if a myriad of smiths hammered out a music". As a crescendo to this swelling music, "great trumpets sounded as if mountain called to mountain".

The dramatic Ella always tended toward such lyrical descriptions, both in writing and speaking, but such passion clearly highlighted her conviction that fairies and their music existed everywhere, for those willing to accept this presence. "It [the music] goes on all the time. It seems to occur or fall silent only because the human receptivity is sharpened, blurred or obliterated." Fairies clearly existed for her many years later in California, as she was trying to become eligible for American citizenship. After much delay and the appeals of attorney friends to the State Department, Ella was finally able to become a citizen of her adopted country. Many people made this possible, Ella admitted, but she gave special credit to fairies, convinced that they played a part and that "the little folk bring good luck".

Ella also encountered elves, creatures that seemed to represent some variation of the fairy; naturally, she had walked and conversed with them. To Ella, the differences between fairies and elves seemed unimportant, although she once described the latter as follows: "They are about the size of a child twelve years old. Their heads are large for the size of their bodies. They have pointed ears, round eyes, and an engaging grin." Ella noted that they had an impish quality and they could "play tricks on people", but she called them "friends" and remembered how they had helped her on one occasion. It was in a "very faery-haunted" place that Ella was joined on her stroll by "five or six elves of the hillside ... trotting beside me". After conversing with them, she asked for their assistance in finding the direction back to her inn. They led her to a marsh, but Ella reminded them that she could not walk across the boggy, treacherous field. The elves insisted that she would not sink into its depths – and she didn't. She walked as though along a pleasant path, and then they bid her goodbye at the highway that would lead her to her lodgings.

There was another mischievous elf Ella never actually saw, although she knew he existed. She called him "Gilpin", borrowing a name used by Sir Walter Scott for a goblin. Gilpin manifested his presence by making things disappear and causing Ella immense frustration and long searches for everyday items. She was convinced that Gilpin played tricks on her by moving such things: "Silver spoons, books, door keys would desert their habitats and re-appear on a cushion, a bedspread or a rug." He was not necessarily a creature of the West; he might appear in Connemara, and then again in Dublin. Ella never felt that lack of seeing him meant he didn't exist. She learned his ways:

> Now when I go to my library shelf for a book of ballads that should be in place third from the end, and find that book gone, I do not hunt frantically about the room in the hope of coming upon it. I just sink into the most comfortable of my chairs and say: "Gilpin, bring back that book!" I give him a few minutes before I saunter to the bookshelf. The book is there!

When Ella shared such happenings with the more earthbound and literal-minded citizens back in Dublin, her accounts were not so much astonishing in themselves as for the very ordinary way she reported them. Ella spoke of her experiences with fairies and magic as though commenting on the weather or planning dinner. At a Dublin gathering during her years of regular forays into the West, Ella held the party spellbound with tales of eerie spirits and strange happenings. She told them about a young boy whom she saw trudging a country road in great pain, with an arm and shoulder half ripped away. He had been attacked by the Water Horse of a certain lake: "You see, he had always been unfriendly toward the horse [when passing by] and it had taken the chance to punish him."

When one sceptic asked if the lad had truly expected such a tale to be believed, Ella turned her ethereal gaze on the doubter, as though incredulous that the story could even be questioned. Indeed, the Water Horse was quite real, she insisted, "especially white ones ... for I [myself] have seen him rear his head above the waves with the white foam in his mane and his eyes shining". The image of horses in Celtic mythology crept into Ella's conversations and writing throughout her life. Ella saw white ones as especially mystical, probably through her awareness of a belief that the white horse, a rare find, was a sacred, other-worldly creature associated with special wisdom. She wrote this poem, perhaps later in America, when she lived near the rolling waves of the Pacific Ocean:

> White horses the sea has;
> Dead men dream of them
> Under the waters.
>
> Whiter than moon-fire they glitter
> In a wave leaping shoreward;
> They neigh in the storm-wind;
> They cry to each other,
> White as the levin-flash
> Sudden and splendid.
>
> White horses the sea has;
> Under the waters
> Dead men dream of them."

In the old times, Irish peasants believed that Water Horses were regular occupants of lakes as well as oceans. These wild creatures were known to appear on land also; Ella remembered her exploration of the Cave of the Red Steeds and the horses that local people swore they saw galloping out of the cave's mouth.

Old folks in County Kerry had told her of "the great horses that come out of the sea and do not find the dry land strange under their feet ..." And in that same locale, Ella swore that she heard the thunder of chariots, wondrous vehicles pulled by massive horses.

She never actually saw the chariots, nor the gods driving them, but she imagined horse and driver "thundering along the strand, immense chariots driven furiously: so massive are they and so headlong is the pace that of a surety the horses leaping and straining in the traces must be kin to those harnessed by Apollo".

Sometimes locales beyond the west of Ireland offered such mysteries, as with Ella's encounter with a stone-throwing spirit on the island of Iona, Scotland's version of the primitive West. She and a friend spent a holiday on this tiny island off the coast of Scotland that was, and is, revered as an early Christian community and appreciated for its intricate carved crosses and stones. Ella was probably attracted to it because of the primitive Gaelic beauty and fragments of civilizations long gone. One day on Iona, she and her friend were searching for the prehistoric gravesite of a chieftain, as well as another spot where "bodies of sailors drowned at sea" eventually washed up on the shore.

They encountered no bodies, but as they paused on top of a cliff, they could hear the sound of a pickaxe striking rock, as if someone were hacking away at the bottom of the cliff. It was a sharp, regular noise that cut the air and punctured the silence of a tranquil Sunday afternoon. Ella was still enough of a Presbyterian to be indignant that someone would do such work on the Sabbath. Then they heard another sound, "a great burst of baying, as if many deep-throated hounds bayed together", and still later, the heavy crunch of gravel beneath a huge man's feet. Intolerable on a Sabbath, they thought, and they set out to find the source of this human and canine racket, but no matter in which direction they looked, the sounds remained elusive.

Suddenly, near the sounds of the pickaxe, a huge stone shot out below the cliff, "crossed a little river, and lay on the grass beyond it". Ever attuned to otherworldly occurrences, Ella marvelled at the appearance of this stone, "one that a man could hardly lift".

When she and her friend made their way down to the river and
approached the stone, they found no mortal nearby. Ella noted
that the stone was not smooth like a beach stone, but rather it was
"sharp-edged, weathered ... one side of [the stone] had lain em-
bedded in the earth", presumably for a long period of time.

What giant had thrown the massive stone? Ella reached back
into her lore and remembered about the spirit who dwelled atop
one of the mighty Cliffs of Moher that loom high above the ocean at
the edge of County Clare. According to the old man who related the
tale: "[The spirit] would sit there all lonesome by himself and pass
the hours of the day casting stones into the water to pleasure himself." Ella also considered a more Christian option: "I remembered
missionary tales of heathen devils that had a resort for themselves
in a grove of trees and cast stones at converts on their way to
church." Whatever the source of the stone-throwing spirits, they
were, for Ella, a further sign of life in another dimension, if only
more mortals could become sensitive enough to enter that world.

Tales of the magical West – and of places like Iona – always
preoccupied Ella. In bringing to life the stories and the people of
those regions, Ella undoubtedly glorified some of her experiences
and some of the people beyond a realistic viewpoint. To her, the
locals who befriended her and gave her shelter in their farmhouses
and villages were all models of simplicity, spirituality and kind-
ness, and were decidedly superior to the more intellectual, albeit
spiritually numb, people on Ireland's urban east coast.

Yet, if Ella found western folk to be nearly perfect and country
living idyllic, this did not mean her journeys westward were all
sublime experiences. Brought up in a servant-staffed home, she
sometimes found herself in accommodations where she had to tol-
erate "linoleum and ... dingy stuffed chairs". On Achill Island, in
the summer of 1915, she referred to roughing it with a friend and
doing much of the cooking: "Everything we eat is brought living to

the door." The most challenging dinner delivered to her was probably a lobster, "a fearful and wonderful creature". It crawled about until Ella returned it, alive, to her hosts, explaining that she had become "too intimate with it to think of eating it".

At times, she was bored and felt isolated from Dublin's urban pace and intellectual stimulation, particularly when the most dramatic events of Ireland's struggle for independence were unfolding there. When storms and wind confined her, not an infrequent occurrence in Ireland, she would become restless: "When one can't go out, one can't talk politics either, and that is a deprivation." She also noted: "The arrival of the postman is a great event." Her sense of separation probably led her to write what seemed to be promotion letters for Achill, urging Dublin-based friends to visit her. She tried to lure one friend there with a description of her house "perched on a green slope that goes down to the sea on a rocky cove … there should be good swimming". Ella gushed over the "flowers of very rich cobalt blue" and the "women in red petticoats and bright kerchiefs", while also extolling the reasonable costs of turf, butter and eggs.[1]

As rumblings of war shook Dublin, gathering native lore was not always the main reason for Ella's journeys. A year before the 1916 Easter Rising, it appears that she fled Dublin because she was on a British "black list" of suspected nationalists. As preparations for war intensified, the British presumably considered her suspicious, because letters she wrote from her retreat in Achill arrived at their destinations in envelopes marked "opened by censors".[2] Was this an indication that British authorities tracked Ella's

---

[1] From one of several letters to artist Estella Solomons, whose Dublin studio was used as a hideout by rebels.

[2] Two envelopes, one dated 23 March 1916 before the Easter Rising, and one dated 23 March 1917, suggesting that Ella fled Dublin during this period because of her rebel activity.

movements and wanted to check her correspondence for clues of traitorous activity? They surely knew about her association with Dublin's artists, most of whom supported the rebel cause.

Beyond political considerations, the cost of living in the city often kept her away: "I don't know when I'm coming to Dublin. I want to be there, but it seems more and more impossible to [let rooms]. Here one is sure of a turf fire ... and some food." Well into her fifties, Ella appears to have supported herself, although only modestly, with her Celtic books and with lectures here and there.

The West of Ireland gave her a wide repertoire of stories and a lifetime appreciation for Ireland's magic and lore. Yet, despite economic and political pressures, and her love of country people, Ella felt the call of Dublin, her home base, and between westward journeys, she would return there to immerse herself in the creative fervour of the Irish Literary Renaissance and the political intrigues of the independence movement.

Chapter 3

Yeats, Maud Gonne and George Moore's Green Door

"I lived there [Dublin] in the most splendid time."

In a dim Dublin hallway on a rainy spring night in 1902, Ella watched the rehearsals under way for performances of the old Irish saga, Deirdre, the cherished legend of the beautiful woman who chooses a young man over a powerful king and meets with a tragic death. On the rough, dimly-lit platform masquerading as a stage, two brothers, directors Frank and Willie Fay of later Abbey Theatre fame, drilled nervous young performers to repeat lines in endless tedium. Their words echoed in the gloomy space, and further back, sitting in the darkness on one of the crude, hard benches, Ella critiqued the progress, along with two friends of the Irish cultural movement: writer George Russell, better known as AE, who had written this adaptation of Deirdre, and activist Maud Gonne, who had supplied many of the actors. AE's voice emerged from deep within his shaggy beard and bounced from murmurs of approval to grunts

of dismay, as words from his scrawled pages took tenuous form among the actors. On the other side of a flimsy room divider in the makeshift theatre, the clink of billiard balls competed with the sounds of rehearsal.

The door behind them slammed, and in breezed poet William Butler Yeats. Even in this modest hall, the dramatic WB made his presence known, rustling his cloak and spraying rain drops from his umbrella as he settled onto the bench with the others. Yeats had just crossed the Irish Sea the previous night, returning from England, where London theatre mixed Victorian drama, comic opera, musical comedies, and farce, much of it presented on grand stages in chandeliered halls. This dim little room in Dublin intrigued Yeats. He sat in uncharacteristic silence – briefly, then bounded to his feet and proclaimed: "This is what I have so often thought of – a theatre drawn from the people. Ah, but that is not how they should speak the words!" He sprang up and onto the platform to give Frank Fay a few pointers on improving the performance. Fay was not amused, and Yeats slumped back to his seat. "I must write a play for these people," he grumbled, "for this theatre. But why do they stand that way? They lose the effect."

Maud Gonne persuaded him against issuing another edict to Fay. As the rehearsal broke up for the evening, Yeats collared the Fays in a final attempt to make his point, until AE manoeuvred Willie away from the brothers, and everyone sprinted toward the shelter of a waiting tram car.

Always attuned to the particularly revealing tale, Ella later re-corded this slice of the mighty Yeats' personality, along with tales of other members of the Irish Revival. Many of her contemporaries would become famous, or at least recognised, for their work in unearthing native Irish stories and in advancing the cause of Ireland's independence. Even though Ella ultimately found her home and her major publishing success in California, she always treasured the Dublin years and noted: "I lived there in the most splendid time." Yeats and others in the literary revival movement fed her emerging creative spirit, encouraged her to explore the West of Ireland and inspired her writing. They also provided a colourful repertoire of stories about her Dublin experiences, which would later enliven her lectures in America. Ella's stories gave a personal, insider's glimpse of the artists involved in Dublin's early twentieth century revival of Irish culture.

Theatre was the most visible symbol of that revival. Part of Ella's fascination with drama probably sprang from her younger sister, Elizabeth. Ella had only mentioned her briefly in childhood memories, but later referred to Elizabeth as "the actress . . . tall and slender with masses of red-gold hair and eyes that have green and amber lights in them". Ella remembered her sister "[playing the] lead in London ... [in] comedies by Beaumont and Fletcher". In Dublin, she once played the Deirdre role in an impromptu drawing room setting; Ella herself took a small role in her one and only performance before the spotlights.

Although Yeats and the Fay brothers had their differences in that 1902 rehearsal of *Deirdre*, they ended up collaborating on joint performances of the play and of Yeats' own play, *Cathleen ni Houlihan*. In Yeats' production, the title character symbolised the personification of Ireland, a "poor old woman" who is transformed into a beautiful queen once the local peasants commit to helping their country gain its freedom. Together, these productions marked a significant event in the fledgling Irish National Theatre, a long-time dream of Yeats and Lady Gregory. A few years earlier they had laid the groundwork for a theatre that would showcase native Irish culture and "bring upon the stage the deeper thoughts and emotions of Ireland". At the time, drama choices in Dublin were generally limited to English touring companies or local groups that performed heavy-handed melodramas.

The two performances were well received, even amid thin partitions and billiard balls. Yeats found a permanent home for the national theatre in December 1904 with the Abbey Theatre, a venue that dramatically increased awareness of the revival movement.

At the beginning of her own career, Ella saw Yeats as the most dominant voice of this movement, and she enthusiastically absorbed the heady creative spirit of the day, as she saw it in him and in other Dublin intellectuals. When she first met him at gatherings of Dublin mystics, Yeats was already earning some artistic fame in a career that would encompass roles of folklorist, poet, playwright, theatrical producer, and Senator in the new Irish state. However, he was known to exhibit a certain air of aristocratic superiority not always appreciated by Dubliners. One observer acknowledged the Poet's growing stature, but lamented that unfortunately, Yeats suffered from a lack "of healthy, roast beef humanity".

At times, Ella did see him as somewhat removed, and often referred to him respectfully as "The Poet". In the early years of the Theosophy meetings, she had acknowledged him as "a candle of knowledge and a road-showing torch" to Dublin's occult community. But she also knew him as "Willie," the domineering artist who meddled in the Fays' dramatic productions and who pursued her friend, the beautiful Maud Gonne, a Protestant aristocrat and fiery advocate for Ireland's independence cause. For his part, Yeats was often irritated by all those who flocked around the charismatic Maud, including Ella, whom he once called his "bête noire," or "black beast," and complained that she "talks elementary textbooks all day, when she is let, with an air of personal inspiration". Ella was quite aware that Yeats did not always welcome her presence. On one occasion, Ella stopped by Maud's Nassau Street apartment and invited her to accompany a group on a country outing:

> William Butler Yeats sat on the far end of the room with the air of someone who has retired from a controversy. He held an open book in his hand: Poems by John Keats. He was not too pleased to see me, and the pleasure lessened when Maud Gonne consented to accept my invitation.

Over the years, Ella's attitude toward Yeats always included a few hints of disapproval, as in a letter to a Limerick friend, including the cryptic comment: "Yeats becoming so fast the unspeakable." Once, in a critique of Yeats' attempt to do his own adaptation of the tale of Deirdre, Ella agreed with a friend that in Yeats' version, "Deirdre is not Deirdre ... he misrepresents an old Irish story".

On another occasion Ella argued with W.B. Yeats over whether man could control his horoscope and his destiny. He believed that mere humans could not alter their predestined fate, but Ella disagreed:

> ... because I was born in a good Presbyterian family and had predestination drilled into my childhood and made hateful to me. My ungospelled self is inclined to believe that life follows a [random] pattern, conditioned like the pieces of coloured glass in a kaleidoscope.

Yet, if she sometimes saw the great poet as annoying, she was not immune to the romantic aura that surrounded both W.B. Yeats and Maud Gonne in the early part of the twentieth century. They were the talk of social and literary Dublin, and Ella added to the mystique surrounding them, as in her dramatic observations upon spotting them at an art museum:

> These two people delight the bystanders more than the pictures. Everyone stops looking at canvas and manoeuvres himself or herself in a position to watch these two.... Yeats

has a dark, romantic cloak about him; Maude Gonne has a dress that changes colour as she moves. They pay no attention to the stir they are creating.

Ella's memories of them flowed even more lyrically on another occasion, as she saw them on Dublin's Grafton Street: "She has a radiance of sunlight. Yeats ... holds back in a leash a huge lion-coloured Great Dane ..." Later, Ella would note: "These two moved through my life for some years, with a background at times of Paris, at times of Irish playhouses, at times of Irish mountain and pinewood, always with a sense of far-off splendid happenings ..." In such romanticised phrases, Ella revealed a bit of herself as impressionable and star-struck, someone who enjoyed at least the edges of the spotlight surrounding this famous pair.

Shortly after Ella came to Dublin, she began hearing about the famous Maud Gonne, who had abandoned an upper-class lifestyle to join Ireland's cause. Ella resolved to attend one of Maud's lectures, although it took some perseverance to go to what critics derisively called a "gathering of ultra patriots". At the time, although well into her thirties, she was still bound by the rules of her parents' household, where loyalty to England reigned: "My folks [would] certainly never allow me to go by myself." Ella found a "respectable person" – her younger brother – to take her to this presumably dangerous, rabble-rousing event. Her first impressions of the lecture were not completely focused on what Maud said about Irish independence; Ella was initially impressed by the activist's appearance: "a beauty that surprises one ... like the sun when it leaps over the horizon. She is tall and like a queen out of a saga."

At the time, Maud was speaking in halls all around Ireland, France and America, on topics such as her protests against tenant evictions in Ireland's West and Queen Victoria's Jubilee visit to Dublin in 1900. Despite nationalist objections, the Queen did make a state visit, and in one ceremony, handed out candy to 15,000 children in Phoenix Park. Maud had countered with her own "patriot children's treat", an event she said drew 20,000 nationalist children who were all gifted with "sandwiches, buns, and sweets".

Ella worked with Maud in the latter's efforts to teach young Irish girls about their country's past and its destiny through an organisation called *Inghinidhe-na-hEireann* in Gaelic (Daughters of Ireland). Most of the young women, from Dublin's squalid back streets, had seen themselves only as toiling British subjects of the Queen until Maud formed the Daughters of Ireland. Ella noted that it attracted "girls who work hard all day in shops and offices owned for the most part by pro-British masters who could at any time discharge them for treasonable activities". These were young women who took considerable risks to attend classes in Irish history, to learn the Gaelic language and dance their native dances. Ella's role involved teaching children, both boys and girls, the old Irish stories and myths, describing her class as made up of "eighty denizens of untamed Dublin: newsboys, children who had played in street alleys all their lives".

Ella met this ragtag class in a dusty room at the top of a rickety staircase, where the children stood packed into a space too small for chairs to accommodate all of them. The windows looked out on a narrow, slum lane where rumbling carts, vendor yells and other street noises fought for the attention of her students, who ranged in age from nine to eighteen. They stood ready to listen, but sometimes they resorted to fisticuffs if the stories did not hold interest, or if they perceived some insult or poke from someone in the packed crowd. Still, they picked up enough snatches of familiar hero names – going back to the old Celtic legends of Cu-Cullion or Fionn, or to the more modern, real-life patriots Wolfe Tone, Robert Emmet, Charles Parnell. Perhaps the "denizens", in Ella's words, had heard such references in the conversations of parents or other family members whose memories had come down to them through the oral tales of many generations.

As Ella recalled, the children fiercely latched on to certain names, and "as they [tumbled] down the narrow stairway, homeward bound, I heard shouts of: 'I'm Cu-Cullion!' 'You're not – I took it first!' 'I'll fight you on it!'" Then they headed out from the classroom into Dublin's scrappy street fights.

Maud had taken her own risks in making these classes available, but the sheer force of her personality – and not incidentally, her beauty – seemed to protect her from much British scrutiny. But in addition to her political, activist side, Maud held the same mystical views as Ella and quite naturally assumed the presence of spirits everywhere. Thus, Maud came to know the ghost that once inhabited Ella's house, which Maud shared for a brief period. Ella referred to Maud as giving up her own house and putting "her carved oak furniture and other beautiful things" into Ella's residence, where a ghost roamed – far different from the sedate spirit of Ella's childhood. This one was a "riotous and notorious ghost" who, in Ella's words, "banged on walls and doors, slipped stealthily along corridors, and gave excellent imitations of a drunken or rage-mad man stumbling up the staircase".

At breakfast the morning after her arrival, Maud said, "You never told me you had a ghost here". During the night, Maud told her, she felt a cold wind, as though windows were open, but they were tightly shut. She suddenly became aware of the ghost in the room; he insisted on showing her a secret passage and took her to what seemed to be an entrance to this hiding place. But Maud drew back in fear and refused to explore it further; he then tried to explain something to her, and she told him that he "was wasting time here: he should go forward in the spirit world". Later, during the war years, Ella would stumble upon that secret passage to a cellar and use it for hiding weapons for the rebel Volunteers. Did the spirit want both of them to know about a site that could be used to help Ireland in its fight against Britain?

Although Maud was but a few years older, Ella looked up to her as an independent Protestant woman who made her own way in the world, and who forcefully worked for Irish independence. Until Ella left for America, they shared other adventures, excursions, and artistic ventures. When Ella published her first book, *Celtic Wonder Tales* in 1910, Maud created illustrations for this collection of Ireland's best-known stories; the title page bore her pictorial interpretation of "The Children of Lir", the legend of four children changed into swans and sent into exile by the proverbial wicked stepmother. She also illustrated Ella's 1918 book of verse, *The Rose of Heaven*. Ella recalled writing two lyrics for a play (its title not indicated) that Maud produced for Daughters of Ireland.

In more personal matters, Ella was one of those who counselled Maud against her planned marriage to John MacBride, Boer War hero, hard-drinking son of Catholic shopkeepers, and later one of the martyrs of the Easter Rising. It was indeed an unlikely union, and when the inevitable divorce occurred, Ella, along with AE, tried to arrange some arbitration for the warring couple.

In later life, Maud would provide some insight into Ella: "She was an extraordinary woman, frail in appearance, but with an iron will. . . . She was always extraordinarily happy and I loved being with her and missed her greatly when she went to America. She had the gift of making life colourful."

Ella was adept in handling boats; now and again, she managed to snag a sailing boat from a friend to ferry Maud and others from a Dublin harbour to the nearby island of Ireland's Eye. There Ella led them in the ritual of lighting the Bealtaine fire of the old Gaelic festival, a reference to the May first celebration marking the onset of summer. The fires, Ella believed, purified the land after the harshness of winter, and for that ceremony, she used herbs she had gathered from different parts of Ireland to symbolise both the unity of all beings and the unity of Ireland, north and south.

Ella's obsession with unity came, in part, from her leadership of a Dublin group called the *Fine*, possibly a variation on the Gaelic word *fianna*, or group. Ella had founded the organization upon leaving AE's Hermetic Society, which she came to see as not suitable for Irish needs. Maud Gonne remembered that Ella was inspired to start the group "after long meditations on the Swastika and long before anyone had heard of Fascism; strangely enough, also, the salutation between members of the *Fine* was the raising of the hand, almost like the Fascists. Ella said it was the old Gaelic form of salutation."

However chilling the gesture later seemed in post-World War II hindsight, at the time Ella found the salute meaningful for members of *Fine*. Maud explained that Ella's goal in *Fine* was to free Ireland by drawing together "the wills of the living and the dead in association with the earth and the elements which to her seemed living entities". She had chosen the lonely island of Ireland's Eye to represent the earth in Ireland, hence the Bealtaine journeys there to commune with that earth.

The trip to Ireland's Eye was just one of many such pilgrimages that Ella, Maud and various other friends took to what they considered sacred Irish sites. They were especially fond of making journeys to mountains, such as Slieve Gullion Mór, north of Dublin, which they believed was home to special spirits. This was not a lovely peaked mountain, but rather a "humped and enormous bastion" that fronted the Irish Sea. More casual travellers might have seen it merely as a flowery hulk of a hillside, but to Dublin mystics like Ella: "So sacred it was that men, animals and even household goods brought within its shadow were in sanctuary."

Mountains, looming above the fields and mean cottages, had always held the Irish imagination, had always seemed places of mystery close to the gods. Irish mountains certainly did not offer the grandeur of the rugged peaks that Ella would later see in California. However, the Irish version of mountains seemed formidable and powerful to a people who were predisposed to see magic in all of nature. Some mountains were associated with old Celtic myths; Slieve Gullion Mór was said to be the haunt of the great sea god, Manaunaun. This deity possessed the ability to calm the seas or to whip them into chaotic frenzy, and he was revered by the Irish in a land so often attacked by enemies from across the sea. Legend had it that this mountain was also the site where the great mythical hero Finn MacCool received the drink from Manaunaun that broke the spell of the strange woman who had transformed him into a withered old man.

On one such trek around Slieve Gullion Mór, a member of the group told the tale of a woman who tried to invoke the image of a great mountain one night as she lay sleepless. She indeed got a response: "the strong power of the Mountain invaded [her] room and took such whirlwind possession of mind and body that she feared exceedingly and could scarce endure the anguish." Even the mere contemplation of a powerful mountain could bring unwanted consequences, and, as Maud observed: "Sacred Mountains are too strong for mortals; it is like inviting a lion to play with you."

The most sacred of Irish sites was not at a mountain at all: the Hill of Tara, west of Dublin, another destination for Ella's outings. There she could let her extravagant imagination wrap itself around the era of ancient kings who had built fine palaces and ruled all of Ireland from this hilltop. She visualised the poets, druids and storytellers who gathered there for festivals. In Ella's day, Tara was the most potent symbol of Ireland's past glory and of the nationalists' continuing determination to have a land ruled by Irish leaders. In the mid-nineteenth century, it had been the scene of a massive gathering of thousands, known as the "monster rally," an event that drew people from all over Ireland to hear the great patriot and orator Daniel O'Connell speak. He stirred the people to such fervent heights about Ireland's right of self-rule that the British quickly banned all such meetings thereafter.

Ella had visited the site often over the years, but on one particular occasion, the hallowed hill seemed neglected, uncared for: "Tara is a desolation. One has to trace laboriously the foundations of the great banquet-hall, and speculate as to where other palaces might have been." She journeyed there in a party that included Constance "Countess" Markieviecz, the flamboyant Sligo aristocrat and erstwhile wife of a Polish count. She was the only woman who commanded troops in the 1916 rising, digging trenches and holding off the British in Stephen's Green. She was imprisoned but escaped execution, the fate of other rebels, because of her sex.

The Countess provided the transportation to Tara in one of the few cars then on Irish roads. The dramatic Countess, as Ella remembered, drove the party to Tara in a "bright yellow roadster . . . with two Sinn Féin [nationalist] flags flying . . . it ricochets from bump to bump of a road made for horse vehicles". Constance Markieviecz was also among those in Ella's circle who fantasised about reclaiming Tara's most precious treasure: the "Stone of Destiny", or the *Lia Fáil* in Gaelic. On this Stone, according to legend, high kings of Ireland took their oath to rule the people wisely. The Stone could also determine that a man was worthy and destined to lead Ireland; if the right person, according to Ella, "stood with both feet upon the Stone, it gave a deep sound of approval. It roared." However, the Stone had been missing from the Hill of Tara for centuries. As the story went, Scottish kings secreted it away; then an English king raided Scotland and took the Stone to England, where it was secured in London's Westminster Abbey.

As they walked around Tara, they could see the verdant fields below and knew that much of the land still belonged to absentee

Anglo landlords, making this hill of ancient kings all the more symbolic of Ireland's plight. They began plotting the rescue of the Stone of Destiny, arguing the merits of various plans. Of the seemingly impenetrable Westminster Abbey, the Countess mused: "We [the Irish Republican Army] have planned many raids on it. But the place is well-guarded and the Stone is heavy." Still, she fantasised about how the IRA might somehow gain entrance to the Tower, seize the stone, and spirit it up to Scotland. "We might hide it there for awhile," said Gavin Arthur, the American in their group and grandson of the US president Chester Arthur, who had come to Ireland looking for his ancestral home and stayed to take part in rebel activity. Sneaking the Stone onto a boat from Scottish waters, he reasoned, would probably create less British scrutiny than transporting it from England. Ella, however, had her own ethereal scheme about the Lia Fáil: "We might, if we could, make a strong enough spiritual centre, [and] occultly transport that power to Ireland. The Stone [itself] must follow." But the Countess, ever the practical soldier with little patience for such a dubious mystical scheme, felt that only solid action would suffice and would serve to rally the people to the cause for Irish freedom.

Among other friends of Ella's fascinated by the Lia Fáil was the poet and publisher George Russell (AE). One day, she dropped by his house and found him and Yeats in deep discussion about kidnapping the stone: "Yeats had a bunch of grapes in his hand and between mouthfuls detailed an elaborate plan of action." Ella did not give the details of Yeats' scheme, but in truth, all the grand plans and talk of snitching the Lia Fáil were largely symbolic; no one in colonised Ireland seriously contemplated the taking of a famous relic from a guarded British site. But its absence from its true resting place fed the imaginations of the revivalists and became a powerful sign to them of what they considered Ireland's true destiny.

Of all the people in this intensely romantic band of Ella's friends, AE exerted the most influence on her. Never as famous as Yeats, AE arguably affected the literary and cultural movements of the day in far more diverse ways. During his highly productive life, he was variously a poet, playwright, artist, publisher, mystic and an advocate of cooperative farming for poor Irish farmers. Ella was fascinated by this literary and agricultural mix: "[He] ... is as much interested in cows and chickens as ... in gods and elves." He had abandoned the conventional name of George when he came across the word "aeon", used by Gnostics to denote divine emanations from God. Thereafter, he signed all his work with "AE", as a tribute to his belief that all men carried their own divinity within them. With a wild beard, shaggy mane of hair, and hearty manner, he had been known to hold forth in public squares, exhorting passersby to realise that the earth, the ground they walked, was sacred.

Ella had come to know him when he spoke at Theosophy meetings, and she followed him when his circle of young intellectuals broke away from the Theosophists in 1898. When she first heard him speak, she marvelled at his "wonderful voice, unlike any other I had ever heard ... he did not seem to be human, but rather the vehicle through which some Being, rainbow-hued and unearthly, manifested itself". AE's new group formed the "Hermetic Society," a Theosophy offshoot of eclectic spiritual practice that emphasised Eastern mysticism, magic and diverse views of God. AE infused the group's thinking with his study of Ireland's ancient life under pre-Christian forms and undoubtedly influenced Ella's own pursuit of Celtic mythology. Still living at home with her family, Ella regularly traversed the chasm between her family's conventional Rathmines row house and the Hermetic Society meetings at which AE lectured on occultism.

Hermetic members often posted poems and other snippets of writing in their meeting room. One day, Ella found a mischievous poem about her, perhaps written by AE. Or it could have been penned by another writer and mystic of the day, Susan Mitchell, who specialized in satirising Dubliners in saucy verse. Whoever the author, it seemed to be a dig at Ella's lingering Presbyterian certainties about salvation:

> My sister Ella takes of you [God]
> A territorial sort of view:
> I think an island is her notion
> Somewhere in the Atlantic Ocean

It is unknown whether Ella, AE, or any other Hermetic members found anything amusing about the pranksters who once invaded their room at night, after hours. Perhaps none of the Hermetic members knew how a pair of ladies' underwear, draped over a broomstick, appeared in the room one morning. The pranksters turned out to be a very young James Joyce and Oliver St. John Gogarty, the model for Buck Mulligan in *Ulysses*. It may be difficult to imagine the mighty Joyce involved in such shenanigans, but the prank probably symbolised his well-known disdain for the Protestant mystics and for what seemed a dubious aristocratic claim on Catholic culture. He saw Theosophy and its related movements as a frantic recourse for disaffected Protestants and once remarked that Dublin mystics "do not compare either for consistence, holiness, or charity with a fifth-rate saint of the Catholic Church".

Ella's group, with its focus on mystical realms and stories of Ireland's past, existed worlds apart from Joyce's forward pursuit of European modernism in literature. But Ella might well have fit into Joyce's view of Protestant mystics, as she abandoned Presbyterianism for the Hermetics. She faithfully attended their gatherings; however, the main attraction for her came when AE met with several young poets, Ella included, to critique their work. She had been writing long before coming to Dublin, in what she considered the

culture-starved "Midlands" of Ireland, where she "had plenty of leisure [to write] but no one to hearten" her and give her encouragement. AE provided that stimulus, and Ella finally felt motivated: "I
have tried for years to carve something beautiful out of words ... I
am trying harder than ever now ... [AE] gives to me, as he gives to
all his poets in tutelage, much advice. He thinks even, of sponsoring
a small book of verse selected from our best attempts." However,
AE was a tough critic, never referring to any "streak of genius" in
her, a term, she noticed wistfully, that he sometimes applied to others. After she wrote and rewrote her verses and brought them to
him, he replied: "Why don't you get music into them? Sound is
what matters. You should know your Keats and Shelley better!"

In 1904, AE did, in fact, publish the "best attempts" of his students and other up-and-coming poets in a slim volume called *New
Songs*. It seemed that Ella had succeeded in bringing sufficient
"music" into her poetry, because he included several of her poems
in the book. AE's foreword noted his attempt to showcase Ireland's younger poets and "to show some of the new ways the wind
of poetry listeth".

In the book, one of Ella's poems, "The Star of Knowledge,"
foreshadowed her own restlessness and a quest for artistic growth
that would summon her always westward, an urge expressed most
tellingly in these lines, addressed to the "Star," also referred to as
the "Ashless Flame":

> Once face to face with thee Odysseus came
> In the lone island when the gods had hurled
> His ship to ruin on an alien sea:
> And I may reach thee, Ashless Heart of Flame,
> When I have wrecked for thee the narrow world
> Fate built about me, and my soul is free.

The reference to the "Ashless Flame", Ella believed, went back
to the old Celtic festival of the goddesss Brighid, held in February,

symbolising her gifts of poetry and learning. It was also a reference to another festival, Samhain on November first, and the god Mananaun drawing the sword that would split the "narrow world" and bring about beauty and enlightenment. In the early years of the twentieth century, Ella was constantly searching for this enlightenment, for some version of Odysseus' wanderings, whether in the solid form of her subsequent journey to America and California, or in a symbolic spiritual way. It is possible that in this early verse Ella referred to a growing awareness of her lesbianism in a deeply Catholic and conservative Ireland. That awareness could explain Ella's desire to escape "the narrow world Fate built about me". Her writings and the memories of others never referred, at least overtly, to Ella's sexual preferences; given the times she lived in, this silence would not be surprising.

Whatever her meaning, she was encouraged by seeing her work on the printed page. Over subsequent years in Dublin and California, she honed her craft. Her poetic voice would evolve into a more modern twentieth century cadence and depart from such sedate usage as "thou" and "thee". Although her modest fame emerged from her Celtic mythology adaptations, she wrote poetry throughout her life and published several volumes. She came to see the role of the poet as sacred, particularly during Ireland's battles against Britain, viewing all poets as "worshippers of the Holy Earth" at a time when the land she venerated had become a bloody battleground. At other times, she felt despair as a poet; in a letter to a friend in 1920, as the War of Independence raged, she mused: "Poetry especially seems to belong to a world other than this ... when one tries to turn a rhyme, one feels like Nero fiddling while Rome was burning."[1]

---

[1] One of several letters about Ireland's cause to Joseph Campbell, poet, lyricist, patriot, emigrant to America. Ella wrote similar letters to his wife Nancy.

However, Ella was also deeply influenced by the poet-turned-soldier, Patrick Pearse, who had succeeded, she sensed, in integrating the world of poetry with a warrior's realm. He was a poet and teacher long before he became the fiery defender of the rebels' headquarters at Dublin's General Post Office in the 1916 Rising. Patrick (Padraic) Pearse was the son of an English father and an Irish mother; he studied for the Bar but never pursued a legal career once his imagination was caught up in the revival of Irish culture. He joined the Gaelic League, an organisation founded to preserve the language and literature of Ireland.

As a young man, Pearse believed it might be possible to battle the British intellectually. He published old Irish tales from ancient manuscripts and his own poems in Irish, and wrote numerous essays and articles that encouraged his countrymen to seek out their true Irish identity and work to resist English influences. When Ella watched him lecture in both school and community settings, she was deeply impressed: "There is no one who can arouse an audience like he can, yet he speaks very simply and without gestures; some fire in the man himself kindles flame in the listeners."

Clearly, Ella drew inspiration from him in her adaptations of the old Irish hero stories:

> The sagas, the tales of gods and heroes, the poems well-hammered and riveted with assonance and rhyme – these that belong to us, our joy in discovering them, our determination to know them and to make them known, Padraic Pearse's determination that Ireland shall be worthy of them – these are building up our nationhood: these and the Gaelic language.

Ella came to know him even more when she lectured occasionally on Celtic mythology to the "eager, alert" students of Pearse's Irish-speaking school, St. Enda's, which he established in 1908. When Ella first came to lecture, she noted in the entrance hall a large oil painting of the warrior Cú Chulainn. It brought to Ella's mind the old story of this revered hero. Druids had told him it would be ominous to confront the enemy in battle on that particular day, but his name would be well remembered if he chose to go ahead. Cú Chulainn had chosen the battle despite the dangers, reputedly saying: "Though I should live but a year and a day, my name shall go sounding down through the ages." Then Ella noted that the inscription around Cú Chulainn's picture carried those same words in Gaelic. Later, she would reflect on this apt epitaph for Pearse himself, who went on to become the most famous of the Easter martyrs.

Ella found more reminders of warriors in Pearse's special museum room containing old objects from Ireland's past attempts to fight colonial rule: "a cannon-ball from the siege of Limerick; pikes with hand-hammered iron heads that were carried in the '98 rising, swords and pistols treasured once in mountain caves..." At St. Enda's, Pearse tried to instil in his students both Christian values and warrior strength: "I would wish the boys to have the hardihood of Cu-Cullion and the Christ-heart sympathy with all living things."

After several years of promoting these values and preserving native Irish culture, he came to the conclusion that only military force could succeed in throwing off British colonial rule. Ella shared Pearse's staunch determination that Ireland should never compromise in its determination to throw off British rule, and after his martyrdom in the 1916 Rising, she continued to support the civil war conflict set off by the divisive 1921 treaty.

However, in the heady artistic spree of pre-war Dublin, Ella could not imagine the violence that would soon engulf them. The city, at least her community's slice of it, was alive with new theatre and awash in poets, translations of Gaelic stories, and classes in the Gaelic language. Singers and fiddlers entertained the populace in the streets. Lively political discussions raged over pints of stout in the city's many pubs. Ella noted: "It was a Dublin that had lei-

sure to talk at street corners, to be witty about trifles, a Dublin of
sonneteers and raconteurs." Later, she would remember the city's
lighter moments, as well as its artists and soldiers.

One "trifle" of a story sent Ella on a stroll to the house of George
Moore, the witty dramatist who wrote *Hail & Farewell*, a book that
described, none too reverently, the main figures of the Irish Renaissance. Raised in great wealth, Moore was one of the few well-to-do
Catholic landowners. He came to empathise with the native Irish
aspirations, embracing a position that prompted him to paint the
door and railings of his rented Dublin house green.

When Ella came upon his home in Ely Place, an Anglo enclave,
she indeed found workmen applying – not a subtle green – but
rather the boldest, brightest emerald green of Irish patriots, a colour that greatly offended his neighbours and his landlord. Ella
remembered:

> Ely Place was aroused; its railings had never been painted
> green. Green was a disloyal colour, only flaunted by
> misguided rebels and by the commonfolk . . . even as I
> strolled slowly and contemplated this outrage, the door was
> torn open and a man with a mass of untidy pale blonde hair
> came out on the steps and stood there gesticulating to his
> workmen. My first glimpse of George Moore and the
> beginning of the Saga of the Green Door.

Indignant neighbours conferred and pressured the landlord to
intervene. Moore immediately composed a letter to the landlord
and to all the newspapers. In it, he told his critics that his whole
house was, as Ella recalled the letter: "a symphony: Its carpets, its
Manets, its mirrors, its curtains, all were phrases in that symphony, but the keynote was the Green Door!" If he changed the
door, Moore patiently explained, he would then have to change all
his furnishings. Neighbours, not moved by the harmony of his
decorating scheme, responded by hiring organ grinders to play in

front of his house and by encouraging their dogs to bark loudly when passing by. In another protest, two elderly ladies were so outraged that they encouraged their two cats to mate in front of Moore's home. For his part, Moore was said to have hired a pipe band "to play outside their [the ladies'] house at night so for some time no one in the cul-de-sac got much sleep". Ella and the rest of the city relished the fun of watching the standoff: "George Moore made himself as objectionable as he could, and Dublin elaborated [on] the saga." Eventually, the landlord withdrew from the controversy, and neighbours turned their attentions to other matters.

Dubliners were also entertained – or enraged, depending on their sensibilities – by the opening of John Millington Synge's play *The Playboy of the Western World* at the Abbey Theatre in 1907. In the story, Western Irish villagers made a hero out of a young man who had presumably killed his father. The townspeople, who shared an instinctive hatred of the British-affiliated police, hid him from the law. Men stood in awe of his act, reasoning that his father must have somehow deserved the decisive blow on the head, and anyway, they would never turn one of their own over to authorities. On the opening night of *Playboy,* rioting broke out and the largely nationalist audience erupted in boos and hisses, offended that idolised Irish peasants of the West could be portrayed as so lawless and cunning.

Ella, though not among the demonstrators, sympathised with them and thought of all the virtuous folk she was then meeting on her western forays who shared their humble cottages and fairy stories with her. She felt that Synge should never have included a line in the program declaring that his play "represented real life in the Gaelic parts of Ireland, studied at first hand by the author". Ella saw the play more as an "extravaganza, a fantasy," but since the play had been labelled as a realistic portrayal of true life in the

West, she felt that it "behooved everyone who cared for the reputation of his country to show strong disapproval".

Ella followed all the news of this tumultuous opening night. Beyond the presumed insult to Western peasants, many audience members were enraged by the use of the word "shift" in the play, which at that time meant an item of ladies' underwear, a reference thought unacceptable in such a public place as the Abbey Theatre, or even around dinner tables. Demonstrators returned on succeeding nights to voice their displeasure at both the language and the offence to Western Ireland; protection was provided for the actors by "burly, good-natured metropolitan police, each six foot high". As Ella remembered it on the night she attended:

> When the second act came on, the patriots didn't boo. They didn't make a disturbance of any kind. But suddenly the air was full of snuff and pepper. The actors coughed and sneezed; the audience coughed and sneezed; the big policemen wiped their eyes, and didn't see anyone they could arrest. When the actors recovered their voices, they went on where the coughing left off. The objectionable parts were past. Everyone was satisfied. The actors had said the words; there had been a demonstration; no one was arrested.

Ella always treasured such little jewels of Dublin life and made them part of her lifetime repertoire of stories. At the time, she could not have known that the symbol of a patriot green door would soon become more than just a nuisance to Anglo residents, and the "snuff and pepper" demonstrations in the Abbey Theatre would seem quite an innocent way to protest. The city of so much literary and theatrical energy would shortly be engulfed in the violent War of Independence.

Chapter 4

Gun-Running and the Easter Rising

"My grief, Dublin will be burned."

Amid the chaos of civil war and rebellion, on a rainy night in December 1922, Ella Young opened the door of her Dublin flat and found several soldiers on her steps. All were armed with rifles and pistols. They had come, they told her, to search for anything suspicious. Might she have some runaway rebels or weapons tucked away? Ella assured them that no fugitives or guns lurked in the shadows of her closets, but they insisted on seeing for themselves.

Reluctantly, Ella stood aside, and the soldiers all tramped in. This wasn't the first time Ella's abode had been searched. A few years earlier, during Ireland's War of Independence, English soldiers had searched the modest attic quarters that comprised her home at the time. Since then, Ireland had presumably won its freedom through a 1921 compromise treaty negotiated by Michael Collins, but that agreement left six Northern counties under British control.

So, a bitter civil war raged all across the country, pitting Irishman against Irishman, and Ella's friends were the Anti-Treaty rebels who continued to fight for a united country, North and South. On the other side was the new Free State, which grew out of Collins' treaty, and these polite young men searching Ella's flat were Free State soldiers, just doing their jobs. They were invited in by a slim, stately woman in her early fifties, with wisps of silvery hair and thoughtful grey-blue eyes. She watched as one of the soldiers looked under a chair cushion, precisely the place where pistols had been stuffed between the seat and the back, thankful that they were hidden more securely now. "In fact, the flat is an arsenal. Under the floor there are Thompson machine guns, in the false back of a cupboard there are most important papers. In hiding places, ammunition." The soldiers moved on to search her bedroom, pawing through drawers of silky underwear and patting several dresses in the wardrobe, as though a satin evening gown might have ammunition sewn into the hem. Heads down, the Free State soldiers shuffled to the door, apologised to her – and left.

A relieved Ella threw herself into the armchair that had so recently been scrutinised. She hoped the flat would not be searched again, at least until the weapons had been removed by her friends in the Anti-Treaty forces.

The Ella Young who heard fairy music in the hills and dabbled in the occult seemed an unlikely person to guard weapons under floorboards. Yet, she had been involved in gun-running and other rebel activities long before the independence struggles erupted into the 1916 Rising. When Ella referred to living in Dublin in "the most splendid time", she meant more than friendships with William Butler Yeats and Maud Gonne. Even as early as 1905, she noted that "we are all fighting hard" in a letter to a friend, thanking him for sending along some war songs: "mayhaps [they] will cheer us ...", a reference to the need for encouragement against the well-armed coloniser.[1]

During seven centuries of British rule, throughout the country, the Irish people had mounted a few sporadic uprisings and scattered attacks, but England's military always succeeded in rolling back any challenge – usually at the price of bloodshed and death on both sides. The most prominent of these attempts became known as the 1798 Rising, or the "Year of the French", when French forces – long time foes of England – joined with Irish rebels in attacks led by a flamboyant Irish Protestant named Wolfe Tone. Nationalists adopted him as a hero, and his efforts, however futile, inspired the poet-martyr Patrick Pearse who, in turn, inspired Ella Young and others to intensify the battle in the early twentieth century.

Thus Ella's involvement in Celtic literature and oral stories progressed from a love of Ireland's culture to her sense that it was vital to throw off the rule of a coloniser who threatened that culture. Ella never doubted that it would take bloodshed to achieve that goal. In 1914 she came across a prophecy of war in the journal of a rising anti-British republican organisation called Sinn Féin (Gaelic for "ourselves alone"). The prophecy, one that appealed to Ella's sense of story and mystical foretelling, came from a Gaelic-speaking man from Antrim:

---

[1] One of several letters to Seamus O'Sullivan, also known as James Starkey, founder/editor of *Dublin Magazine*, married to Estella Solomons.

He was a man who wandered about the roads and was thought by the country-folk to have the hand of God on him because his wits were troubled. He went from house to house and had bed and supper and a welcome offered to him, alike in small cottages and comfortable farmhouses. One night he came into a friendly farmhouse and said that he had a vision. He wanted it written down because he knew he was going to die.... The prophecy says, "A war will break out about the time of harvest. The English will be fighting in it, and the Irish, and my grief, Dublin will be burned."

At the time, Ella and other Sinn Féin readers may have assumed that the man referred to then ominous signs of impending, inevitable war in Europe. But how could a war on the continent mean that Dublin would burn, in a country that was attempting to stay neutral? Several weeks after the publication of the prophecy, Ella had a vision of her own that reinforced the notion of Dublin afire. She was standing on a sidewalk near Trinity College, waiting for a tram car amid the ordinary flow of Dublin's workday crowds, when: "Suddenly I became aware of the fact that I was looking at blackened and ruined buildings.... I saw gaping windows and piles of fallen masonry." Ella was convinced that she had foreseen the violence of 1916 and the beginning of the War of Independence.

However, before Ella's vision could be fulfilled, the nationalist movement would lose some of its momentum precisely because of World War I. Negotiations then underway with Britain regarding Home Rule for Ireland were stymied, as Parliament turned its attentions toward Europe. Even though Ireland's own battle strategies were consigned to the back burner as World War I began, plans went forward in secret. Around 1915, Ella was clearly involved in the smuggling of arms and living on her own, away from her family. She moved into an "old-fashioned, dilapidated" farmhouse in County Wicklow called Temple Hill, where she and Maud

Gonne had encountered the noisy ghost. Ella had procured the house for a nominal rent after promising the landlord she would refurbish it and repair the overrun garden. In the cellar formerly occupied by that ghost, Ella filled the space with smuggled ammunition, rifles and bayonets.

Ella may have coordinated this arms smuggling with Erskine Childers, a Protestant civil servant who had formerly been employed by the British House of Commons. He left his job to join the Irish fight for independence and became famous for running guns off his yacht to arm the Irish Volunteers. Using Childers' yacht was a conscious strategy by the nationalists, who assumed that British authorities would not suspect a boat designed for leisurely outings. Once Ella's allotment of weapons had been secured in the cellar, it was her job to guard the front door and secure a Gaelic password from any one who approached. When she responded and recognised the caller, he handed her a slip of paper that read: "Give X so many rifles, etc., etc.," and then strong Volunteers would muscle the weaponry up from the cellar and into the hands of rebels.

On one particularly tense evening at Temple Hill, a large car, loaded with concealed weaponry ready for distribution, stalled in front of Ella's house. By lantern light, rebels tinkered with the car and kept an anxious eye out for the local police, an affable group of Royal Irish Constabulary (RIC) members, usually bored, who routinely helped people with "disabled cars and sick bicycles", as Ella put it. Finally, the car shook and sputtered into life and the driver set off with the cache, before police could arrive.

During the months leading up to the 1916 Easter Rising, Ella had opportunities to see not only the RIC, but also the British forces, merely as men trying to do their duty for England, fellow humans who often forgot to see the Irish as adversaries. At the Portobello barracks near her new quarters in Rathmines, which she rented after leaving her Temple Hill home, she observed that many of "the English Tommies for some time past had been leaning over back walls and trading rifles, blankets and other equipment, for bottles of whiskey, pressed on them by eager patriots". During the initial battles of Easter week, another example of man's hopeful, if sporadic, tendency to humanise the enemy concerned a Catholic servant of Ella's mother. The young girl believed that her sweetheart from the country was inside a factory taken over by the rebels, and she begged for, and received, the afternoon off to go see him. At a checkpoint, she told a bored young sentry that her business in Dublin was urgent, that her "mother was dying, and [she] was the only child". Once within the war zone, she made her way to Jacob's factory, one of the battle sites, where the English soldiers presumably attacking the patriots inside were enjoying a rest:

> No officer was in charge. Standing, sitting, or lying, they were smoking cigarettes. She explained to them that she wanted to talk to her sweetheart who had just come up from the country ... "Just bawl his name out!" said one of the Tommies, "and if the fellow is inside, he'll come to the window."

He was indeed in the building, came to the window, and the couple shared a few moments together. Then one of the English soldiers said to her: "Look out and get away from here. We're going to fire." The young girl left her lover who would shortly be fired on by the men who arranged their meeting. If any story could soften the brutality of battle, this one could help explain the conflicting nature of war. Ella, as a Protestant with some familiarity with the British culture, could appreciate such paradoxes and see the humanity on both sides.

However, such flashes of good will were few, and Ella was focused on the ultimate goal. Her own clandestine gun-running comprised one link of a network of rebel activity, aimed at supplying arms for a major, widespread revolt. In the days before the 1916 Easter Rising, Ella seemed to have knowledge of an imminent plan: "On that day there will be a sound of marching feet. Men everywhere are to strike for Ireland's freedom."

She was anxious that all the plans would come off smoothly: "Have cargoes of arms been landed? Have we strong well-equipped outposts beyond Dublin?" She spoke of "cargoes" obtained, again, from Germany, this time by Sir Roger Casement, formerly an official with the British consular service who became a supporter of the Irish cause. Casement accompanied the arms back to Ireland and docked at a presumably secret point on the west coast, but the cargo was captured by a British submarine. Casement was arrested in County Kerry and later executed, delivering a blow to the rebels and their plans. Perhaps Ella had not yet heard the news about Casement's arrest when she expressed optimism about the success of his mission and mused that "he should be with us when the Flag of Ireland takes the wind".

The Easter Rising began on Monday, 24 April 1916, and plunged Dublin into a long week of carnage and destruction as sixteen rebels directed the takeover of several buildings and sites with an army of around 1,600 volunteers. Ella followed the conflict from the distance of her Rathmines neighbourhood on the outskirts of the city proper. She joined the throngs of residents who heard the crack of rifles and the stamp of marching feet, as British soldiers left the nearby Portobello barracks and marched across the Canal Bridge into the city. But no Rathmines residents could venture into the downtown area; all were turned back at checkpoints. Kept a distance from the actual fighting, Ella and her neighbours swapped a steady stream of news, impressions and speculations: "The English have a warship in the Bay!" "They are sending gunboats up the Liffey!" "The Irish are rising everywhere, God bless them!"

Actually, the "rising" that was supposed to occur all across Ireland fell far short of the original goal, which called for Irishmen around the country to take up arms. There was a bit of marching and skirmishing elsewhere, but certainly no "strong well-equipped outposts beyond Dublin", as Ella had hoped. The burden fell on Dublin, mainly with a few patriots in the General Post Office on O'Connell Street where Patrick Pearse and others held off the British as the building burned around them. On Easter Monday, Pearse read a proclamation from the steps of the Post Office, declaring the country to be a free republic. The opening words would become famous in Irish history: "In the name of God and of the dead generations from which she receives her old tradition of nationhood, Ireland, through us, summons her children to her flag and strikes for her freedom."

Stirring as these words were, as the week progressed their impact seemed muted in the smoky, frenetic chaos of battle. Ella continued to hear the sounds of downtown fighting:

> Machine guns are sputtering. Rifle shots, rifle volleys puncture the intermission. There is fighting in the streets. How much or how little, no one can guess. But certainly there are dead bodies in the streets.

Beyond the sounds and the reports, some factual and some not, that drifted into Rathmines, all residents felt the impact of the battle and knew that they were involved despite their distance from the actual fighting:

> Everyone must be indoors by six o'clock. There is a curfew regulation. No lights can be shown. Outside, there is plenty of light, for Dublin is burning! The Post Office is burning, and so are other buildings in the heart of Dublin. A red, a blood-red cloud like a pall.

One week after the Rising began, Patrick Pearse surrendered amid the ruins of the Post Office, effectively signing his own death warrant and those of his compatriots. The bridges were open, and Ella was among the crowds that poured into the city proper to see not only the devastation but to breathe in the palpable air of defeat. She tried to find the words to describe the scene and the mood:

> The story of the Rising comes to one in fragments, in excited whispers, in the machine-gun-pitted houses that stand windowless, yet with a sort of hidden triumph, [they] stonily returned the stares of the crowd, a crowd that has always in the midst of it a hunger and a triumph. "You see that house, Mister?" says a small boy. "They held out there for three days, and there wasn't more than three or four of them in it!"

To Ella, the boy's boast symbolised a mood of "hunger" for some hint of good news and of "triumph" for the fighters who showed determined courage even as defeat was certain. Perhaps everyone had known the outcome, had sensed that this idealistic band of men could not prevail against the might of England's powerful armies and weaponry. Still, Ella felt sure that national pride could not be destroyed by a vastly superior enemy.

Ella enthused that "everywhere among the people there is an awakening, a pride, a joy in the achievement of the undaunted group that attempted the impossible". Later historical accounts would dim the glow of glorious sacrifice in which Ella and her compatriots seemed to bask. Decades after the fervour of that week had subsided, historians noted that the badly planned Easter Rising ultimately took the lives of more civilians than rebels: 64 rebels killed (excluding 15 rebel leaders later executed) versus 318 bystanders and more than 2,000 wounded. Further, the down-town sites chosen for takeover, such as the General Post Office, did not strike at the heart of British occupation at Dublin Castle, the seat of colonial government. As it turned out, there had actually been an attempt to storm the Castle, which failed. Trinity College, with its close ties to Britain, would have also been a strategically better choice, later critics suggested. The College was virtually empty of people during Easter rituals and might have been easily captured.

Aside from the group of fervent nationalists that included Ella, the Dublin populace was generally furious, not only about the loss of lives and property, but also about the disruption of normal routine such as mail delivery at the embattled Post Office, where wives went to collect money orders from husbands fighting in World War I. After a week, many parts of downtown lay in rubble and the stark skeletons of buildings still smoked. Ella noted that "someone was bold enough to plant the Sinn Féin flag on the blackened and gaping roof of the General Post Office". She also watched the inevitable looting: "... men, women and children staggered under fur coats, damasked armchairs and bales of silk. Diamond rings and jeweled watches were sold on the streets for little more than the price of a drink." In the days following the Rising, some rebels were roughed up and pelted with tomatoes by angry Catholic citizens.

However, the British decision to execute the Rising rebels soon turned the tide of public opinion by enraging an otherwise indifferent populace and arousing indignation over the deaths of fifteen patriotic Irishmen. (History records 16 rebels executed, which includes arms smuggler Roger Casement and excludes Eamon de Valera because of his American citizenship.) The news of these deaths would help set the nation irrevocably on a course of war against Britain, but aside from skirmishes and isolated attacks, the more formalised Anglo-Irish War did not begin until 1919.

Throughout the conflict, Ella often found herself at odds with her British-leaning parents. She once asked a friend to forward her contribution to the "men who are making such a splendid fight", and she requested that her name not be attached to the money because "my people would object so heartily". She was still in contact with her family, but she had definitely departed from their tradition of loyal allegiance to England. Thus, when her name showed up on a British "black list" of dangerous nationalists, she took her own gun, a small pistol she had kept for defence, and turned it over to her father, lest it be found on her person. This genteel Protestant writer who lived a life of the spirit in the company of Gaelic gods and mountain fairies grew increasingly militant in her views as the conflict continued. A letter to a friend at the height of fighting urged unwavering dedication to a long struggle and warned that association with the British Empire is "deadly" and that "[we] must purify ourselves to be worthy of an Ireland fought for by martyrs". She spoke of the dangers of allowing the coloniser to continue subverting Irish heritage.

However, her determination went far beyond the liberation of Ireland into an idealistic vision of a whole new order in the world: "I see that we must overthrow this civilisation and this social system. They are things that destroy beauty and sow hatred between man and man." She was intrigued by the Russian Revolution, noting to a friend: "Aren't you glad about the Bolshevik successes? Russia, Ireland and America are the three nations destined to bring in the New Age." Ella was among many patriots who followed the news of the Russian Revolution, identifying with a fight seemingly similar to the Irish struggle against an entrenched power. Ella's language often took on religious tones, urging her fellow rebels to "... preach the gospel of it [Ireland's struggle] to enlist recruits everywhere.... We are fighting for the new order in the 'New Age'." With such sweeping conviction, Ella was decidedly unsympathetic with friends who had any contact at all with the British. When she heard that her old friend, historian Standish O'Grady's wife Margaret, had served tea to British soldiers during the Rising, Ella vehemently disapproved: "I fear the O'Gradys have got on the wrong side."

Shortly after the Easter Week attacks and the executions of the rebels who had planned the rising, Ella left Dublin for a period of time. She seemed to have fled because her rebel activity was attracting British attention. Probably in 1917, she went to her beloved West of Ireland, to Achill Island, hardly a banishment, but still a lonesome distance from the monumental events and the shifting news that was more available on Dublin streets than in western hamlets. She also stayed for some time in Waterford, south of Dublin, where extended evenings of fairy music in the hills distracted her from the independence movement in the aftermath of the Easter Rising. Still, she felt isolated from events in Dublin and complained of the lack of stimulating conversation in a "sleepy Rip Van Winkle paradise".

She was back in Dublin by the early part of 1919, once more involved in rebel activity, this time from a "respectable" pro-British residence, "the garret room of a tall, old-fashioned house that looked out over a city" where her quarters sheltered "a little store of ammunition ... well and carefully hidden". One night, in this "quiet, decorous residence-house", where framed photos of English royalty and members of the military adorned the front parlour's mantel, British soldiers mistakenly raided the house and enraged the pro-British landlady. At Ella's attic door, a soldier courteously told her that he "must search the room ... [but then] just flashes the searchlight around ... and departs with an apology for troubling me". The soldiers were probably searching for a much more substantial stash than Ella's "little store of ammunition". She surmised that, back at headquarters, the men would be thoroughly reprimanded for searching the house of one of their own sympathisers.

Ella appears to have lived in several Dublin places during the war years, such as the aforementioned attic quarters. She tried to find "lodging in rooms" that were within the budget of a modestly paid writer and lecturer and often seemed to be searching for a place, showing some urgency about this quest: "I *must* let a room as soon as possible [italics mine]." When she was living in the attic quarters, Ella observed from her window a city still convulsed with the upheaval of war: "Dublin is filled with excursions and war alarums.... Patriots have been murdered in their homes. Dáil Éire-ann [the renegade government set up by the rebels] has declared a state of war to exist between Ireland and England." By this time, war had been formally declared and was no longer concentrated in Dublin; Ella heard "news of fighting in streets all over Ireland".

This was the period of the "Black and Tans," special groups of British police reinforcements, some of whom were veterans of World War I, and others who were mercenaries and soldiers of fortune, those always lured by the thrill of battle. Often called in to retaliate against IRA attacks, they were both hated and feared by the Irish, who came to feel that any presence of the Black and Tans meant either capture or bloodshed, or both. From her window one evening, Ella was observing the lights-out edict that went along with the six o'clock curfew: "If a light shows in a window, a Black and Tan fires, haphazard, at it." Secluded in darkness, Ella watched a group of Black and Tans in the street below guarding two IRA prisoners, presumably waiting for an officer. When he did appear and gave the order to "March!" the group moved down the street:

> They fall in, two and two, the soldiers in the middle of the column.... They move with echoing steps on the deserted sidewalk. Now they are close to the mouth of a little lane,

dark and crooked. The soldiers pass it, heads erect, in fine marching order, but the two prisoners dart into it like trout into a rock fissure.

Ella then heard shooting, as the Black and Tans retraced their steps and tried to find the captives in a maze of lanes, "firing as they run. Other soldiers in the distance answer them: soldiers from behind walls, soldiers from house tops". The shooting stopped and the Black and Tans straggled back onto Ella's street – and to her relief, without the prisoners.

On at least one occasion, Ella played a more active role in an escape when she accompanied a group that was escorting two IRA captains, who had just broken out of prison, away from Dublin so that they could join their fellow rebels south of Dublin. The idea was to make the trip look like a festive Sunday outing:

> We donned our best Sunday clothes and gayest hats and set out in the car ... laughing and chatting together [with the captains].... Other citizens were going south in cars and trying to forget that a war was on. Every now and then we encountered lorries and patrol cars, but we kept a good face on things. No one stopped us.

Their good mood dissipated in the town of Enniscorthy, where news spread that the Black and Tans were making a house-to-house search, and Ella's group worried that there would soon be a cordon thrown around the village. Ella suggested that the group take the captains to a point where they could make an escape ("they knew the country well"), while she stayed behind to counter any questions that might arise from searchers. As it happened, the Black and Tans left town before completing their house-to-house mission; "they scrambled into the lorries and hurried away, followed by the muttered curses of the populace", well after the young IRA captains had fled deep into the woods and found their units.

Escapes from the Black and Tans did not always end so happily, and the war continued with attacks, counterattacks, raids, searches and appalling loss of life. Finally, international pressure (including that of the US government under President Woodrow Wilson) and a military stalemate led to the January 1922 Treaty – the one Ella so despised – that stopped the bloodshed, but divided Ireland. She and her Anti-Treaty compatriots were happy with "no more burning villages, no curfew, no rattle of musketry in the streets", but they were suspicious of the agreement and vowed to stay "keen-eyed and unrelaxed".

During both the War of Independence and the Civil War, Ella joined other women nationalists in the organisation Cumann-na-mBan (the Irishwoman's Council), a women's auxiliary formed to aid the war effort. They were determined to perform in more than any meek, secondary capacity. They made it clear that they wanted to work in the most active and militant ways possible in a society opposed to seeing women in the front lines. Few women managed that feat. So most learned to drill and shoot rifles, and they prepared bombs, cartridges and bullets for battle. Many women acted as dispatch workers, or "basket girls", walking or biking to take messages and food to the garrisons, often through dangerous territory. But their missions were largely successful, as British soldiers were not inclined to suspect members of the fair sex out on seemingly innocent errands.

It is not clear whether Ella ever participated in these activities during the war. But in the aftermath of the Treaty, she was among citizens sent around the country to see how various communities were coping with the new, and controversial, compromise agreement. Ella went to County Kerry at the request of Erskine Childers, friend from the old gun-running days, to bring details of the treaty and to "learn on the spot of local conditions". Ella accepted the assignment happily, seeing it also as a chance to visit her beloved West: "I shall talk with many resourceful patriots. I shall have a chance to gather folk-lore: a chance to hear traditional singing." In Kerry, Ella found that the residents, of "keen and experienced fighting stock", were settling down to the business of peace, even though everyone was troubled because counties in the North remained in British hands. As always in the West, Ella felt the presence of spirits, this time unfriendly ones: "... some malicious entity tried hard on two occasions to knock me out [discourage her] just before a very important meeting, but I got help", presumably from spirits more sympathetic with her mission.

Soon, any semblance of a mass accommodation to the Treaty faded, as the Anti-Treaty opposition, especially Eamon de Valera, its leader and survivor of the 1916 Rising, gathered enough forces to fight the new Free State government. Civil war broke out in the spring of 1922 and the weary country was again plunged into conflict, this time among Irishmen. Ella approved of the military action: "Words, arguments, impassioned oratory – it will take more than words to decide this issue, there is blood and bitterness of death in it." She was convinced that Irishmen should not accept anything less than total freedom and unity. Her image of Ireland's glorious fighters as descendents of famed warriors of the past led her to support continued bloodshed. For Ella and those who shared her romanticised view of martyrdom, the whole struggle, beginning with the actions of the Easter rebels, had always been a splendid sacrifice for Ireland. "I think it is not peace that we are striving for," Ella said in a letter to a friend in 1920, "it's the right to be what God made us – what we believe God intends us to be."

Looking back on the tumultuous events of that era, it is easy to find fault with both the idealistic, flawed planning of the Rising and the glamour of martyrdom that Ella and others seemed to indulge in. She said of the executed Patrick Pearse, "his mother must be proud of him," and she recalled his exhortation to work "for both a free and a Gaelic Ireland". To Ella, Pearse always exemplified the ultimate ideal in patriotism and sacrifice: "... it is only bit by bit that we see how great he was and what a marvelous thing his gift to Ireland is." Ella was also impressed by the work of Arthur Griffith, who co-founded Sinn Féin, the organisation that gave frustrated patriots a voice and a rallying point for rebel activity. She credited Griffith with creating an atmosphere of determination not seen since the days of Charles Parnell. However, when Griffith helped negotiate the compromise Treaty with Lloyd George in London, Ella felt conflicted about a friend who seemed to betray the cause. And yet, Ella knew that Griffith desperately wanted to end his country's bleeding and do the best he could to continue working toward a united Ireland.

More destructive than the War of Independence, the Civil War that followed ultimately took the lives of 800 troops, on both sides, and thousands of civilians. Around 12,000 opponents of the Treaty were interned or imprisoned. By the summer of 1922, Ella was aware that "prison yards – no longer in British hands – were crowded, and overcrowded, with Irishmen whose only crime was championing their country". Some later historical accounts stated that Ella herself was imprisoned, but accounts vary on that score and on any possible prison term she might have served.

It pained her that the Irish were fighting one another when they had previously been united against a single enemy. In December 1922, shortly after Free State soldiers searched her flat, she mourned the execution of four main players among the Anti-Treaty forces:

> No wonder the sky was lowering and black. No wonder the Free State officer [in charge of the executions] was shamefaced.... This is not a treachery of the English government. It is the work of Irishmen, some of whom worked and fought in company with these murdered men.

Finally, in May 1923, de Valera called off the hostilities, and some semblance of order began to take hold in the fledgling Irish government, although murders, burnings and kidnappings still continued. In following years the IRA kept up a campaign of resistance against the British government, mostly in Northern Ireland, although major violence has now ended thanks to lengthy, on-and-off negotiations among nationalists, Unionists and Britain itself.

Unlike some of her Free State Dublin friends, such as AE and Arthur Griffith, Ella fervently believed the sacrifice of life was worth continuing the bloodshed in the Civil War, but ultimately, she and other Anti-Treaty advocates had to live with the outcome. In the spring of 1924, Ella focused her energies on a new project: a committee set up to establish a fitting memorial for all Irishmen who gave their lives for the cause of independence. This would take the form of a richly illustrated vellum book inscribed with the names of all those who died for the Republic since the 1916 Rising; poems and sayings from the martyrs themselves were to be added. Ella's involvement seemed to include some fundraising letters for the project; each appeal included a copy "of our prospectus which has just come from the printer". Ella also referred to events that benefited the project: "The idea of the Book is being enthusiastically received on all sides and every entertainment organised for it has been a remarkable success."

As the new Republic, minus six Northern Counties, took root, some artists and writers in the 1920s, '30s and beyond found one aspect of the regime intolerable. The Catholic Church, always a pervasive presence in Irish affairs, succeeded in influencing the new government to impose some heavy-handed censorship on literature and art. In the coming decades, many Irish writers – including Brendan Behan and Sean O'Faolain – would feel the pressure of that heavy hand on some of their works.

Ella, whose airy adaptations of Irish legends were designed mostly for young people, never experienced the weight of censorship, but she did become increasingly disillusioned as she saw the division of her land become an accepted fact. She began to turn her attentions across the Atlantic to the country that had lured so many Irishmen in the nineteenth century. She did not leave Ireland for political reasons entirely. A new challenge awaited her in America, where she continued her journey westward.

Chapter 5

The American West, Splendid as a Lioness

"... a land lean-ribbed and austere ... golden-eyed and languorously alert"

In 1914 in Temple Hill, the rambling County Wicklow, Ireland, house with its resident ghost and cellar full of arms ready to place into rebel hands, Ella responded to a gentle tap on the door and found a gypsy on her doorstep, a woman whose family had surely come, at some ancient time, from the Romany tribes of Eastern Europe. Her face was lined and leathery from years of wandering through the Wicklow hills. She said to Ella, in words that conveyed a pointed priority: "Put a piece of silver in my hand with good will, and I will tell your fortune." Ella obliged, and the gypsy predicted something Ella never thought possible: "You think you will live here pleasantly for a long while, but you will leave it in a short time very suddenly. You

will cross the Big Water, and in the country beyond it
you will have more luck than ever you had here. You
will end your days across the water." Ella thanked the
gypsy and went about her work of hiding weapons and
adapting old Celtic legends. America would have to
wait.

At the time of the gypsy's prophecy, Ella was a published author of Celtic mythology and also a lecturer in the subject at
such venues as Trinity College and the Irish Literary Society. The
Irish independence push was simmering on the back burner of the
nation's political life, while a full-scale world war was taking hold
on the Continent. Engrossed in both her art and her rebel activities when the gypsy appeared, Ella had given little thought to the
vaunted land of America that continued to lure thousands of her
countrymen to its shores. She had heard a bit about a wild, wide-
open place called California: "When I thought of America as a
child, I thought of the Falls of Niagara and of California, but
chiefly of California!" Her childhood picture of the Golden State
probably resembled that of children of many cultures: "full of
cowboys and mining camps and gold-diggers and gold mines,"
even though such adventurous images were fast becoming history
on America's West Coast. Her more literary images merged Bret
Harte stories, Joaquin Miller poems, and "tales of giant trees and
deserts", although all of these images seemed the changeable day-
dreams of a child. As a young adult in Ireland, her goal was simply
the far reaches of Ireland's Atlantic towns and farms; clearly a
broader view of the West would soon open up for her.

It wasn't until 1922 that Ella seemed to give any indication of
her interest in America. In a letter to her friend Joseph Campbell,
a fellow nationalist and poet, she promised that "if I go to Amer-

ica, I shall certainly speak of you", a reference to helping him set up lecture tours, once she had established herself. Ella's own American opportunity came along in 1925, when a New York agent offered to book lecture tours for her along America's East Coast and possibly beyond, aimed at an audience that included thousands of Irish immigrants and their descendents who were either homesick or simply nostalgic for contact with Ireland. There was a sense among California friends that her old friend, Gavin Arthur, grandson of the twenty-first president, used his influence to bring her into the United States on a temporary visa.

Ella was both flattered by the agent's interest in her work and disillusioned with the political state of affairs in Ireland, with the compromise Free State government in power. It was time to leave, and even at age 57, when many Irish women might think of staying close to a safe, familiar hearth, Ella again looked westward for new adventure. She journeyed by train to Queenstown (now Cobh, County Cork) at the southern tip of Ireland, the harbour from which millions of immigrants far less privileged than Ella had set out in the dank, dark lower passages of ships, determined to endure the crossing and find fortune in America.

While Ella had been raised to take comfortable surroundings for granted, she was still somewhat disenchanted with the ship that she boarded in Queenstown harbour. In no way did it measure up to her romanticised pictures of "tramp steamers and freighters". Instead, she travelled on a "well-equipped, indeed over-equipped, liner ... a big hotel!" Ella's reverence for Nature, for the spirit life she sensed in land and sea, led her to mistrust the luxurious atmosphere of her ship: "With a blare of dance music it churned across the Atlantic, shedding garbage and ashes on every wave that lifted a head within reach." However, it is likely that she managed to enjoy the comforts of the trip.

Any misgivings Ella had on the voyage quickly disappeared upon arrival in America, as the liner moved past "a group of giant buildings that thrust starkly from the water, sky-devouring, incredible – the City of New York ... strange as those fabulous cities that sprang into being at the word of a magician ..." Even though Ella later felt more at home near the lonely Pacific Ocean dunes than anywhere else in America, New York City held a powerful attraction for her. Her reaction was not so different from that of the hordes of immigrants who flocked there after the famine and even into Ella's day, the rural peasants who gaped awestruck at the city's mighty skyline and the Statue of Liberty. However, as a writer with a lyrical command of the language, Ella was better able to express the splendour and sweeping scale of New York:

> I have seen this city crouching with its canyons under the stars.... I have seen it a-glint with sunlight that does not warm the thought of it, as sunlight warms in one's mind the thought of other cities. It is born without father or mother. It reminds one of nothing save itself.

She revelled in the city's dynamism and energy, sought out its museums, and endured snow far different from Ireland's "slowly-descending flakes", finding herself in a blizzard that "blots out the sky and the sky-reaching New York houses. It whirls itself and whirls me."

Ella started her American tour at Columbia University and then journeyed all along the East Coast, drawing in audiences with the help of a brochure created by her agent, showing on its cover the headline, adapted from Peter Pan: "Do you believe in fairies?" The accompanying photo showed a slender, middle-aged woman gazing into the camera with a soft, ethereal look. Later, California friends would struggle to describe a gaze that seemed to penetrate other worlds and realities.

The brochure went on to describe the subject of Ella's lectures, under such titles as "Celtic Ireland and the Story-tellers", "Nature Magic", and "Fairy Lore", based on her experiences among Irish-speaking families "in peasant huts, in fishing boats, and on mountain sides. They are living stories, still real in the lives of the simple people who relate them." Ella always seemed respectful of West of Ireland people who not only told her stories, but also took her into their homes. Her own words in the brochure conveyed a deep appreciation for people she considered to be keepers of centuries-old legends:

> If I have anything to interest an American audience, it will be because I have lived in wild places amongst a primitive unspoiled people, and have heard by turf fires in little mountain cabins stories a thousand years old, and tales of faery creatures that happen amongst such people even now – and because I have myself a heart that loves such stories and such adventures.

Ella's ethereal air sometimes created the impression that she lived solely in the world of spirits, giving little attention to practical matters of life and career. However, she astutely built her reputation as storyteller and writer with flattering endorsements from major literary figures in Ireland. Her old friend Maud Gonne gushed about Ella: "She is so penetrated by her subject that the heroes and heroines of Celtic legend become living things to her listeners." Joseph Campbell called her "one of the best of the women writers of Ireland" with a "quiet dynamic power" as a speaker". On the wave of such lyrical compliments, Ella lectured in Washington DC, Boston, and on college campuses, stopping now and then for a bit of sightseeing at famous American literary places, such as the homes of Longfellow, her mother's favourite, and poet Amy Lowell. Remembering back to her infatuation, as a young girl, with Louisa May Alcott's *Little Women,* Ella also vis-

ited Jo's house, so named for the strong-minded character and
one of the four sisters in the novel.

During these first months, Ella seemed to regard her stay in
America as temporary, unaware that she would soon embark on a
westward adventure and never return to Ireland. She had arrived
in the late autumn and revelled in the East Coast foliage of "flam-
ing reds and yellow", but felt that this aesthetic experience was
temporary: "If I can see it [America] only once, I choose to see it
now, as I do, in the Fall." At some point on the lecture circuit, Ella
decided to cross the country and continue her westward thrust to
California, where she had some appearances arranged. Still, she
thought it would be only a matter of time before she journeyed
back to Ireland.

Along the railway route, she decided to stop overnight at the
Grand Canyon, having prayed beforehand: "O God, Fates, whatever you are that throw the dice, let me not leave America without
sight of the Grand Canyon." Tellingly, Ella's plea addressed both
the Fates and the God of, presumably, her old Presbyterian days.
When she actually saw the canyon, Ella noted that her literary
skills were inadequate to describe it: "My heart rejoiced in the
Grand Canyon, but I have no words to tell of it – words in the face
of that Marvel are dead leaves whirled on the wind; bat-cries in a
measureless abyss!" In typical Ella fashion, her inability to capture
the canyon's essence was itself couched in highly literary language.

In the face of doubts about her time in America, Ella found
ways to stay on, and, as the gypsy predicted, she did live out the
rest of her days in the United States. She seemed to embrace the
land completely, even though she had loved and fought for Ireland
so passionately. She adopted her new country with much the same
zeal, using the metaphor of a wild animal to express what seemed
to her a nation of restless, pacing energy: "This country is a lioness, tawny, alert, passionate, austere, a beautiful, splendid – per-

haps terrible – thing!" What did Ella mean by the word "terrible?" Perhaps she felt that the sheer size of America and its robust grandeur, particularly in the West, could represent danger even in its wild beauty. Immigrants from all cultures were lured by the promise of American success, but in reality, Irish newcomers often found cruelty and discrimination – and physical danger – in the workplace. Clearly, Ella was not among those desperate post-famine arrivals from Ireland, but she knew that a lioness, while beautiful to watch from afar, can pounce suddenly and tear dreams apart.

Probably in 1926, as Ella travelled across the country, she saw in physical form the symbols that attracted immigrants: the rolling acres of farms unfurled across the continent, cities pushing up skyscrapers, and miles of factories fuelling a giddy, can-do economy still more than three years away from the great market crash. Yankee optimism vibrated across the American landscape as though on telegraph wires. Ella drank in this environment both on the lecture circuit and from her train seat as she headed westward. Sometime shortly after her arrival in the country, she penned a poem that captured her view of America, one that incorporated her image of the lioness and differed markedly from some immigrants' gold-in-the-street dreams:

How could I know, America,
Hearing you praised for bigness,
For opulence alone,
As a calf is praised for the market,
How could I know you a land
Lean-ribbed and austere,
Splendid as a lioness
Golden-eyed and languorously alert?

In this poem Ella's view of America seemed particularly focused on the western United States, on the "lean-ribbed and austere" scenery of the Grand Canyon, New Mexico and parts of California. She saw the vibrancy of the country not in material terms, but in a "golden-eyed and languorously alert" dynamic that marked both the landscape and the Western artists she met in her travels. The "splendid" lioness lured her across the country, away from the tidy fields and towns of the East Coast, just as the West of Ireland had called to her from the settled city blocks of Dublin. She once commented that, next to Ireland, "America was the most magical place".

When Ella set out westward from the East Coast, her destination was San Francisco. A mix-up in changing trains sent her to Pasadena by mistake, an error that she accepted quite philosophically, especially when she gazed on the "orange orchards and roses and palm trees". Her response to the error carried echoes of that long-ago arrival in a tiny West of Ireland train station, where no one greeted her as expected and where she simply set out walking, sure that "some adventure [awaited]". Several adventures did await, at first in the form of travel around California and lectures at an eclectic assortment of venues. Ella noted: "My manager ... gets engagements for me up and down the coast, and as she has no one else to manage at the moment, she drives me in her Buick from place to place." In those early months in California, Ella was not well enough known to command appearances at major halls or universities, yet she was quite happy going to "out-of-the-way hamlets where a nobler-minded celebrity would not think of picking up a lecture. We go [to such places] because the countryside is handsome, or has wild flowers on it, or a lake – or any good excuse for gladdening our eyes ... new mountains, new fields, new byways."

Ella's memories would seem to have exhibited little concern over making money, leaving the impression that she was content to cover expenses and have a bit of pocket change left over. However, in her late fifties, she was advancing her career, as evidenced in the two books published before leaving Ireland and the storytelling reputation that had initially attracted a New York agent and brought her to America. There is no evidence that American or Irish patrons financed Ella's efforts, although some sources suggest that US scholars who heard her speak in Dublin may have eased her way into a University of California lectureship. Still, it is instructive to view her travels and independent decisions through the lens of early twentieth century realities; Ella Young carved out her own story at a time when most women could not imagine crossing the Atlantic or travelling the California coast without male protection, nor following what modest opportunities presented themselves, never knowing if income would continue to flow for the next month, or the next year.

As she became better known in California, the pace became more frenetic; she would find herself "speaking often at only one school or one club in one town and then rushing on". Because Ella's books were read by many young people, she was frequently invited to classrooms to tell fairy tales to children. Ella's willingness to adapt to any unexpected event served her well on the lecture trail. On one occasion she arrived at a Catholic academy expecting to lecture on Fate, in its Greek, Norse and Celtic versions, to eighteen-and-nineteen-year-olds. In addition to that expected audience, however, all the younger academy children were on hand eager for fairy stories. Quickly, Ella had to merge a few engaging, attention-getting tales into what had been planned as a more adult, scholarly discourse.

Ella often sought out audiences of children. An early friend and admirer in California remembered the time that Ella joined a horseback caravan to tour Central Coast sites. After several hours of rugged riding in mountainous terrain, she decided to rest at a local library and sent the rest of the party on ahead. When her companions returned, they found her telling "Irish hero tales to spellbound little listeners" whom she had collected in the library's reading room. She always remembered the advice of her friend, the poet Padraic Colum, on holding audiences, and his warning that "dead knowledge" never suffices. Over the years, for groups of all ages, Ella learned to see her lectures as "living things born of the moment, taking form and substance from my listeners as well as from myself".

However, the pleasures of the lecture trail dimmed after a few months, and Ella finally settled for a while in a community called Halcyon, near San Luis Obispo. The wandering lecturer, who had first seen California as one more stage of her American trip, noted to a friend in an April 1926 letter, "I may be able to stop over the summer and autumn here". That stopover extended to more than thirty years, mostly in the San Luis Obispo area, with snatches of time spent in Big Sur and seven years as a lecturer at the University of California at Berkeley.

Regardless of her actual mailing address, Ella always seemed at home somewhere near the Pacific Ocean, perhaps because she found reminders of Western Irish nature all around her. Ella's tributes to Nature (always capitalised in her mind) and its spirits spanned the California coast, including the promontory of Point Lobos in Big Sur, which – in some mystical circles – had a reputation "heavy with memories of heathen ceremonies and potent incantations . . . [a place] to be approached with caution". Ella and a party of friends stopped there one day on an outing and found a mysterious tidal pool "which flashed with the many-coloured splendour of a Nature Spirit. . . . At the bottom of it the image of a great serpent lay coiled in stone." Ella greeted the spirit in Irish and felt much of the heaviness of Lobos dissipate. As in Ireland, she felt in touch with the spirits of pool, or stone – and mountains.

Over the years, she made pilgrimages to Mount Shasta north of San Francisco, with its imposing twinned peaks that dominated the landscape for miles around. Ella, who readily saw all moun-

Elizabeth, Ella's actress sister

Ella in Dublin – photo used on back cover of Celtic Wonder Tales *(1910)*

Art by Maud Gonne in Celtic Wonder Tales *(1910)*

ELLA YOUNG

IRISH POET
SCHOLAR
AND STORY
TELLER

Do You Believe
in Fairies?

Ella Young knows all about the fairies and fairy
doings. She has read wise books on the subject;
and talked with those that know. Old peasant women
have whispered to her of mysterious disappearances
and weird silences. Young men and brides have
told her strange dreams. Old men have taught her
incantations. Boys and girls have told her of wild
adventures and of wishes come true. Little children
have told her of eerie playmates and magic lullabies.
And the fairies themselves have told her things.

▽

Exclusive Management of
WILLIAM B. FEAKINS, Inc.
Times Building, New York

Front cover of promotional brochure for American lecture tour (c. 1925)

Ella Young's home, Cluan–Ard, in Oceano, California

Gate of Ella's house, probably a tribute to her last book, The Unicorn with Silver Shoes

Ella in New Mexico (c. 1930)

Portrait of Ella Young, Southwest, 1929
Photograph by Ansel Adams

Art by Maud Gonne – Ethaun from
"The Golden Fly Tale" in Celtic Wonder Tales *(1910)*

George the Evangelist,
one of the Dunites

Gavin Arthur, Dunite and grandson of US President Chester A. Arthur

Poet Robinson Jeffers and his wife Una

Sketch of Ella, probably in her 60s

*Mabel Luhan, Lincoln Steffens,
Ella Young and unidentified man,
Carmel, California (c. 1935)*

Ella Young with Virginia Adams, Southwest, 1929
Photograph by Ansel Adams

Ella, probably in her 70s

Portrait of Ella by Irish artist John O'Shea

tains as sacred, made the journey to commune with Shasta's spirits. On one Mount Shasta trek, she visited there at Samhain, the old November first Gaelic festival from which the Christian All Saints Day developed. To Ella, Samhain was "greatest of the old Celtic Festivals, this Feast of nuts – the Nuts of Knowledge – and of apples – the Golden Apples of the Tree of Life", the source of a grand tradition and the beginnings of a Halloween celebration now a ritual in many countries. The night before their trip to Shasta, Ella and a friend stayed in the town of Yreka and observed the American Halloween ritual, "masked children so joyously and unknowingly commemorating in America a Gaelic Festival". Ella recalled an Irish Halloween fifteen years earlier, with youths rapping on doors, wearing "masks and straw disguises; songs in their mouths; old folk songs", and for their reward, they took away "each an apple and a handful of nuts, and the farmer gave to each one a piece of silver". The US version, Ella must have noticed, was much more a tribute to the Hershey chocolate company than to any ancient tradition.

Ella and her friend followed the more traditional ritual the following morning, the day of Samhain, when they trekked to Mount Shasta, "which we revered as a Sacred Mountain", as sacred as any Irish mountain. There, they stood awestruck at the might of Shasta, at its snow-lined peaks and clouds drifting along its heights, appearing to Ella as the realm of spirits. To honour those spirits, "we lit a small ceremonial fire ... and brought away some twigs of cedar that the Mountain had blessed". Over the years, Ella would in some way observe all four of the great Celtic seasonal festivals: Lughnasa in August; Bealtaine in May; Brighid, goddess or saint in February; and Samhain in November.

Ella was always matter-of-fact about such rituals and about her beliefs in other-worldly beings. She recalled her past lives in Ireland and Egypt. She firmly believed that trees and plants had conscious personalities, and she took it for granted that animals had psychic powers unavailable to humans. Ella saw a distinction between Irish and American spirits; the latter, she insisted, were "different from the Irish, but they are just as friendly, although they are greater. They are more untrammelled. The first to greet me [in America] was the Hudson River. It has such a free flowing spirit, so generous ... and travelling to Omaha I greeted the spirits of the plains, golden and mighty." As with Irish spirits, Ella conversed with their American counterparts, despite the fact that "it was some time before I could get them to answer. I think because they have been left lonely for ages."

She had a theory about the time it took to reach American spirits, opining that it took some effort to make contact, as opposed to Ireland, where "people have [long] had communications and dealings with that other world". Since she herself had had years of experience in such conversations, she was sure that with diligence, everyone could experience at least some form of communication; if they cared enough, and were patient enough to listen, they would eventually make contact.

Once, in a San Francisco Bay Area radio interview, Ella talked easily and at length about establishing such communication with trees, animals, mountains and oceans, asserting that she had no special powers in these areas at all. She outlined a step-by-step process in creating a friendship with, for instance, trees. "It's easier to start with a tree ... [it's] the easiest to make friends with.... Do it by sending out love." Ella explained to the radio interviewer – who was either completely in sync with her beliefs or overcome by a strong mix of intense curiosity and scepticism – that she herself had become friends with a particular tree by first approaching it with a simple greeting "without an idea that [I would] get something ... [I would simply] say complimentary things." Eventually, the tree began to answer her, and they became fast friends.

If trees were relatively easy to communicate with, Ella confessed, mountains were another matter entirely; it was "hard to establish a relationship ... I once spent a year greeting [one] before I got a response," a reference to Mount Shasta in Northern California. However, she found it easier to approach Mount Tamalpais in Marin County; she was even able to hear "fairy music there".

She described to American listeners her memories of a lengthy encounter with an ocelot in the Dublin zoo, prior to her emigration to America. She wanted to know this sleek creature, but he kept to himself, so she kept saying mentally: "Let me see you." Eventually, he came out of his den and finally spoke to her, asking if he could possibly lick her fingers. One can visualise radio listeners as Ella talked so breezily; perhaps they laughed, perhaps envisioned a slightly demented Irish woman, or perhaps they simply envied ways of communication far beyond their comprehension.

Beyond Ella's adventures in California's mystical sites and her tales of nature conversations, her circle of friends was widening to include leading artists and writers of the day. On one occasion, in a car trip down the winding Big Sur highway, Ella was among a group that included the poet Robinson Jeffers and his wife Una, and Mabel Luhan and her Native American husband Tony (New Mexico friends, in California on a visit). They were on their way to a picnic at the site of Jeffers' Tor House, then under construction, the now-famous retreat and legacy of the poet. She described Jeffers, the quintessential nature poet, as "silent with the secret smile and shining eyes of one to whom the wild extended more than a prodigal's welcome". Undoubtedly, the mythological bent of Jeffers' poetry resonated with Young. She grew close to the Jeffers over the years and said of them and many others in her adopted American community: "We have slid together like beads on a string!" One of those "beads", Una Jeffers, later shared some impressions of her friendship with Ella, remembering her on more than one drive down the coastal highway, when Ella was:

> ... kneeling in the dust of the road trying to succour a wounded snake; hovering on the seat at my side as I drove a long car down that terrible old coast road. Our friends who owned the car sat in an agony of apprehension, but Ella peered and pointed into the chasms at our side, following a hawk's flight, as carefree as if she too had wings.

On another occasion, Una remembered the presumably frail Ella on an arduous mountain trail, as others "stopped to pant and take breath, and marvel at Ella, tenuous as a wisp of smoke drifting slowly but steadily to the top, and urging Tony Luhan to send out his Indian calls to echo against the mountain".

Apart from friendships, there were occasional brushes with well-known American literati. At a luncheon near Carmel, Young encountered Lincoln Steffens, the muckraking journalist, and the writer Sinclair Lewis, author of scathing novels about what he saw as America's slumbering middle class; he attracted her attention with his "contumacious red hair and an ironic smile". Sinclair Lewis also told her that he saw Ireland as a white unicorn and asked her how she saw America. "As a tawny lioness," Ella replied, harking back to her poem about America. The symbol of the "tawny lioness" became a favourite expression of Ella's and described her affinity for the western United States, both in her California residence and her visits to New Mexico.

Soon she would come to see herself as an American, although she always related to friends and associates as an Irish lecturer and storyteller, an advocate for Ireland's freedom, and truly an Irish artist-in-residence for the State of California. In the pattern of most Irish immigrants, she never planned to return to her native land, and as far as records show, she never did. But Ireland was always the subject of her writing and teaching. She believed that the cause of full independence depended on Irish-American support and once wrote to an Irish rebel friend that she could do more for Ireland from afar than at home. Certainly, her lectures made Californians more aware of Ireland's culture and its struggles. She may well have sent funds back to her homeland to support ongoing rebel activity in Northern Ireland; many Irish immigrants did so after achieving some measure of success in America.

After five years in California and before her teaching stint at the University of California, Berkeley, Ella visited Canada for the purpose of re-entering the United States with a work visa and the intention of applying for United States citizenship. Until that time, she had periodically applied to immigration authorities for permission to remain in the country for short intervals. In one plea to officials, Ella argued her case by noting that too few European lecturers ventured beyond the Mississippi River, and that deportation would deprive California audiences of her Irish stories. And in a 1930 letter to a friend, she noted that she might even return to Ireland, rather than live with constant concern about being shipped home.

In her rambling autobiography, *Flowering Dusk*, Ella did not spell out the details of her Canada adventure, but she may have qualified for the visa under a British-Canadian quota. Ella's birth in County Antrim – one of the Irish counties still under British control – no doubt qualified her. If that were true, Ella must have shuddered more than a bit at the idea, given her hatred of the colonial presence still in Ireland.

But there were other problems in re-entering the United States. She encountered a "timid and very conventional" American Vice-Consul in Vancouver who saw her as frail and somewhat elderly (she was 63 years old). He doubted her ability to make a living and feared she would become a burden to the American government. He demanded that Ella produce more information about the royalties she received from publishers, and he also stated, according to Ella's version of events, that "Celtic mythology was not a subject to be interesting and my power to hold an audience was likely worn out".

Ella spent several months in Victoria and continued to fire off letters to attorney friends back in California, seeking their help. They, in turn, sent letters to the State Department on her behalf, noting her pre-eminence as a Celtic mythology expert and the teaching position awaiting her at UC Berkeley. Librarians across the country also wrote on her behalf. By this time, Ella had a certain following among American intellectuals, San Francisco Bay Area society and lovers of Irish culture. The incident caused a minor political flap, even prompting reporters at one of President Hoover's news conference to ask: "Now, about that Ella Young case ...?" But no presidential action was required, and officials finally concluded that she would not become a beggar on American street corners. So she headed back to California, applied for – and received – American citizenship, and settled in at the Berkeley campus. Yes, she conceded that friends had helped make her re-entry into the United States possible, but she was also convinced that other-worldly creatures had played a part.

Her teaching position was set up through the university's Phelan Memorial Lectureship of Celtic Mythology, named for James D. Phelan, a former mayor of San Francisco, whose funding, it was bandied about campus, had come from some shady political deals. Before beginning the series of public, non-credit lectures, Ella gave several campus talks to students and faculty only, to promote interest in Celtic studies on the Berkeley campus. Devotees of Irish culture and students from other colleges came from various points in the San Francisco Bay Area to hear her public lectures. A former student who went to Ella's lectures "week after week" remembered that it was not unusual for up to 500 people to fill the auditorium to see her, and eventually Ella's events took place in a larger location. In a spirited Gaelic storytelling style, she recounted tales of Irish mountain spirits and fairy lore, and of the modern Irish writers and Dublin wits she had known.

Ella always began by bowing to the audience and to the mounds of flowers on the table from which she spoke. Then she launched into a repertoire that included "Halloween among the Celts", "Dublin Salons", "Dublin Wits", plus more instructional topics, such as "The Art of Storytelling" and "Craftsmanship in Poetry". "The audience would sometimes ask her to read from Gaelic books", her former student said, "and [people did not know] what she said, yet it was music, and she held us under a hypnotic state." Another Ella enthusiast wrote that Ella's impact on audiences was "deliciously disturbing ... [like] the wheeling of white gulls against thundering skies". Such gushing tribute was typical of some artistic reviews of the time, but she was indeed as much dramatist as writer. She once noted about her teaching: "I do not write my lectures. They are born between myself and my audience."

Ella had a fine sense of theatre and played the role of Irish Druidess to the hilt, clad in flowing, full-sleeved academic robes, both in the classroom and at her Berkeley home, where she often invited lecture attendees in – presumably for conversation. But Ella more often held court, reading poetry – her own or from other Irish poets – and talking well into the night. She lived in what had been a "tattered and derelict" house on Mosswood Road that she fixed up with the help of friends and students. It had been vacant for some time, but Ella saw charm in its ruin and its overrun gardens. With typical flair, she had the inside stairway painted a tangerine orange with turquoise blue woodwork, created a lily pond in the garden, and installed an aquarium of exotic fish. Visitors once found her on her knees in the garden, catching ant eggs to feed her fish.

Ella also spent time in San Francisco, giving community lectures and visiting old friends photographer Ansel Adams and his wife Virigina. She made the journey across San Francisco Bay first by ferry boat and then by the Bay Bridge. In 1937 a friend drove her across the daring new Golden Gate Bridge, a structure she likened to Egyptian pylons. Of her car trips, Ella always referred to friends driving; most likely, she never learned to drive. But she managed to get rides from friends and fans who clearly enjoyed the company of one of Ireland's premier storytellers. Announcements about her would pop up now and again in Bay Area papers: a lecture on Irish mythology at the St. Francis Hotel in San Francisco or her appearance at a William Butler Yeats exhibition at Mills College in Oakland.

By 1936 the funding that paid for her lecture series had run out, and it was announced that Ella Young's appearances would cease. Then letters of protest and letters with checks began flowing in – more than $900, a considerable sum in the 1930s Depression days, and the lectures continued for one more year. But her time at Berkeley had always been considered temporary, given the terms of the Phelan lectureship.

Since arriving in California in 1926, Ella had roamed the coast, worshipped at the foot of Mount Shasta and enjoyed the academic stimulation of a great university. Throughout those years, she still snatched periods of time to spend in another part of the American West: New Mexico.

Chapter 6

New Mexico: Indian Dances and Taos Artists

"This stone-pure, mountain-guarded land is one after my own heart."

A long time ago, a Navajo Indian told Ella, there was a man who knew all the tribe's most powerful songs, and it was a great tragedy when he was killed in a battle. Tribe members tried to retrieve the songs by fasting and calling out to the man's spirit. This spirit appeared to them and said: "In that spot where I died, I will sing to you the songs. But you must come; you must make a ring of power. You must give me power to sing." They hurried to the site of his death and again fasted and waited. Soon the spirit arrived and sang the songs that had been lost, songs that the tribe treasured long after.

As a way of trading good stories, Ella told the Indian this tale: "In Ireland there was a great song once that was lost and the poets fasted; they came to a place where the singer of that song died and for three days and nights they fasted and prayed for him to come." Ella assured the Indians that the man returned and "recited the great song from beginning to end ... in our old books we still have that song".

Shared stories of lost songs helped Ella feel at home in New Mexico -- partly because of an eerie desert landscape teeming with spirits, but also because of the bond she experienced with the Native American tribes in the area. She visited New Mexico periodically during the late 1920s and early 30s and saw it as a place "that possesses like Ireland, the ancient magic". Ella discovered striking, but not surprising, similarities between the old Celtic myths and the Native American stories. She also discovered a new community of like-minded artists in Taos and embraced the whole New Mexico scene with an immigrant's enthusiasm. New Mexico was a revelation for an Irish woman accustomed to the white European communities of Ireland and in most parts of America. For the first time in her life, she encountered a mix of cultures: Native American, Mexican, the dominant white population, plus traces of the old Spanish influence – going back centuries to the conquests of Spain.

Ella found herself in New Mexico because of the famed photographer Ansel Adams. Ansel and his wife Virginia invited Ella to accompany them to the Southwest, where he had a photography assignment. They enticed her with a trip in an "open car" and the promise of "mountain-peaks, desert immensities – the Grand Canyon itself", which she remembered from her train trip across the Continent on her way to California. They also said that she would surely pick up lectures in Taos or Santa Fe or Albuquerque.

But it was the scenic impact of the state that first caught her imagination and opened up her vision of the American west. From the road, at sunset, New Mexico loomed before her as "a faery country all rose and violet, showing itself miraculous and sudden as a mirage". In a short time, Ella seemed ready to abandon California, describing what she saw in ever more extravagant prose: "This stone-pure, mountain-guarded land is one after my own heart: it reminds me of the stony reaches of Western Ireland – of Connemara where the white horses of faeryland thrust untamable heads from wine-dark shadow-encompassed mountain tarns ... I shall stay here as long as it will let me stay."

One of her first impressions was that horses seemed almost as numerous as people in New Mexico. "Navajo Indians ride on horses: everyone in this country of rose and amethyst rides on a pinto, a buckskin, or a golden-brown horse. I mean to ride on buckskin, mule, burro, camel or llama – even a unicorn if the country possesses one!" The term "Native American", of course, was not in use in Ella's day; her references were to "Indians", used here to fit in with her conversations and experiences of 1930s New Mexico.

Given Ella's reverence for Celtic lore and nature worship, it was natural for her to embrace the dances, songs and customs of the Indian culture. She readily accepted its reverence for four mountains known as the Pillars of Heaven. The most dramatic peak, and the one most familiar to Ella, was the Turquoise Mountain, "double-peaked like Mount Shasta – the Sacred Mountain of the Navajos", but more prosaically named Taylor Mountain by the Americans, for President Zachary Taylor. Navajo legend maintained that the mountain was fastened to the sky with a great flint knife.

Ella revelled in such bits of lore and she also delighted in the special foot races of the Taos Indians, in a ceremony designed to strengthen the sun. It came after an unusually long period of darkened skies, and after the tribe's priests and wise men had been consulted. Crowds of Indians gathered for this competition between two pueblos: the women and girls gathered on balconies and rooftops, dressed in every hue of reds, greens, blues, purples. The male racers, each team marked by feathered head-dress and painted bodies, darted across the course; the team who won the most sprints was victorious in the race and presumably made the sun come out during periods of cloudy gloom. When that ceremony did not completely do the job, then a dance around a huge fire, with young maidens and young men moving in opposite rows around the blaze, gave the sun further encouragement. Unsurprised, Ella noted: "Next day the sun came out."

The incident seemed an echo of a long-ago incident in Ireland: a West of Ireland outing on a rainy, gloomy day. Although it was raining heavily at eleven o'clock in the morning, just prior to a noon outing, Ella was not deterred: "I ask my friends, the Nature Spirits, for a fine day. They promise it ... At twelve o'clock the rain stopped."

Ella was not surprised by these obliging moods of weather, nor by the antics of a fierce desert wind during the Buffalo Dance at San Ildefonso Pueblo, home of the Tewa Indians. The power of the Southwest wind was always a potent force in the desert, Ella learned, "able to lift columns of sand and gravel almost sky high". When she and her party reached the plaza where the dance would be held, the wind whipped at the faces of all the "white Americans," until they were forced to take refuge in their cars. But curiously, when the dancers took their places in the Plaza, in the roles of buffalos and warriors, the wind backed away and allowed the dance to proceed. At intermission time, as the visitors again ventured out of cars, the wind lashed out and did not recede until the dance resumed. "The Whites were greatly impressed," Ella mused,

"I heard them muttering things about nature-magic and strange coincidence." But Ella believed there could be no coincidences in such events; in her view, the malicious wind must surely be a subversive act aimed at the coloniser of Indian country.

She learned to distinguish the different cultures among Indian tribes, including the Zuni Indians, a once powerful people who had possessed seven rich cities. Through the changes of a modern world and struggles with the white culture, they were reduced to one. But when Ella visited there for the tribe's house-blessing ceremonies, she found the people prosperous when compared to other tribes, living in high-raftered homes, with industries of "fawn skins, woolen garments ... flocks and herds, fields heavy at harvest time".

The Zunis' elaborate house-blessing rituals made the Irish version seem quite placid. "Here was a religion that all my life I have longed for, perfect, generous-handed, touching the fringes of the oldest myths, laying a finger on the great dreams of the visionaries, bringing the tang and savor of another world." As a balance to this rush of spiritual ecstasy, it should be noted that Ella may have witnessed a ritual performed largely for tourists and resident *gringos,* with the private Zuni ceremonies reserved for members. Still, the tribe has held onto its traditions and mythologies longer than many other Southwest tribes.

Ella remembered sitting in a large, high-raftered room with three altars, bird symbols painted on them. Singers, dressed in ornate garments and bird masks, chanted the Zunis' Myth of Creation story in a hypnotic flow of voices that actually flowed on for a week. As with every culture, New Mexico's Zunis had their own version of how all life came to be, their own Adam and Eve stories. It seemed to her that their chanting was like the sound of the sea. Again, she found herself comparing New Mexico and its Indian rituals to Ireland: "It reminded me of Gregorian chant and of the old traditional music in Ireland, something of another world."

The chanting, she soon learned, was the fanfare for the entry of the gods from the mountain, and as these gods appeared, they began an emphatic dance of "slow, austere, compelling rhythms", figures in bird attire and some in human form, their bodies daubed with reddish brown ochre. The dancing grew more frenzied and intricate, as the ceremony moved from one house to the next. The owner of each home must heed the gods' commands – when to plant corn, to reap the crops, whatever the gods directed. Throughout, Ella keenly felt the Irish connections, seeing the Indian gods as "kin to ... Gaelic Bird-Gods, splendid-coloured".

So consumed was Ella with the exotic ceremonies of New Mexico natives, she may not have noticed that some Indians, whom she found so compatible with her Gaelic culture, were subservient to a dominant white culture, and that years of battles with Mexico, Spain and America had decimated many once-powerful tribes, removed them from their lands, and corralled them into designated areas. Did she make the connection between the plight of New Mexico tribes and the native peoples of Ireland whose land was occupied by colonisers? During her time spent in Taos, she had surely heard about the infamous "Long March" of 1864, when 3,000 presumably uncooperative Navajos of the area were rounded up by the famous scout and Indian fighter, Kit Carson, and forced to walk 300 miles to a small, barren reservation. In modern times, the tribes have varied in levels of prosperity, but in general, poverty and its attendant problems have continued to plague the New Mexico Indians. But in her day, when most mainstream Americans tended to dwell on either exotic images of Indian dances or the villain role of Indians in Western movies, Ella may not have focused on the less appealing realities of Indian life.

Beyond the Indians, Ella became aware of the Mexican population, people who had spilled over Mexico's border in search of work. Occasionally, she rode by horseback on "rutty lanes past Mexican villages tawny and vacant-eyed in the sunlight, past Mexican farmhouses, crouching behind irregularly planted orchards well shut in by adobe walls", which allowed mere glimpses of bright flowers and wide-eyed children who ran out to see this strange white woman in their midst. During one Holy Week, Ella watched the Mexican villagers observe Good Friday and carry a life-size image of Christ to a chapel yard, accompanied by "wild beautiful music". Again, Ella may not have been aware that the Mexicans were as impoverished as most of the Indian tribes.

At this Good Friday service, the Mexican Catholics were joined in a Passion play by *Los Penitentes,* known around Taos as a mysterious secret order of Spanish Christians, not connected to the Catholic Church. *Los Penitentes* expressed their devotion to Christ by practicing self-flagellation, beating their own backs with whips. Ella had watched them march in long lines from their various prayer houses in the desert and the mountains to the chapel yard. They appeared to her as "hooded figures, black as the black shadows, the flagellantes who have prayed and scourged themselves night after night in Holy Week". The self-destructive rituals of some members dated back to medieval times, and it was said that in the past – in the more extreme groups – that one *Penitente* each year would consent to sacrifice himself and actually be crucified. On this occasion in the chapel yard, no such horrific event occurred. This unlikely gathering of *Penitentes* and Catholic Mexicans hung a figure of Christ on the waiting cross and reenacted the sound of nails pounding through flesh into wood.

Ella clearly came to New Mexico on more than one occasion; she spoke of the University of California, Berkeley granting her a leave so that she could spend time reflecting and writing in New

Mexico. Thus, her memories also included attending a Mexican Midnight Mass on Christmas Eve (without the *Penitentes*!), a more joyous occasion, as the Virgin Mary was carried under a canopy to the sounds of violins.

If the scenic beauty and the mix of cultures made a strong, aesthetic impression on Ella Young, so did the community of artists and intellectuals who gathered there from all over the country. At the time of Ella's visits, in the early 1930s, well-known writers, painters and thinkers were flocking to New Mexico to work or rest in the peaceful desert and enjoy the company of like-minded artists.

Ella came to know Mabel Luhan, the New York heiress and cultural historian, who enthusiastically promoted Taos, New Mexico as an arts center, who embraced the Native American culture wholeheartedly, and who married a Taos Indian. She grew up in a wealthy, privileged Buffalo family, but came to reject that lifestyle and to see the mainstream American culture as dangerously obsessed with striving and individualism. She opened up her home to countless artists and encouraged them to establish their own creative bases in Taos. Thanks in part to her efforts during the first half of the twentieth century, Taos became a mecca for artists and would-be artists, those searching for both inspiration and a lifestyle hopefully more authentic than that offered by what they saw as a stifling American consumer culture. Partly because of Mabel's hospitality and her zeal about the artistic advantages of the Taos community, D.H. Lawrence and his wife Frieda established a home there, as did Mary Austin, who gained fame as a writer of western life and landscape. It was said that Mabel lured D.H. Lawrence to Taos by sending Indian jewelry, blessed with charms and spirits by her Indian husband Tony, to Frieda.

At one of Ella's lectures in Santa Fe around 1929, Mabel clearly bonded with Ella's spiritual Celtic outlook and swept her back to Taos as a houseguest. Mabel's home was known to many guests as the "Big House", a term that must have resonated with Ella through her memories of the Protestant "Big House" in Ireland, the symbolic reminder to many native Irishmen of the Anglo landlords in their midst. Mabel's house was a much more rustic affair, sprawled on a plateau below Taos mountain, supported by massive pine trunks. Doves cooed in the central courtyard, and cocks on the roof-edge – "yellow and green, and scarlet, and rose-velvet", as Ella remembered them – crowed each morning. Ella stayed in a guesthouse, one of several adobe dwellings, all adorned with intricate Mexican furniture, all housing Mabel's entourage of artists. Ella seemed not to mind a lack of some modern conveniences; light came from oil lamps and the glow of candles, and the telephone was "safely hidden in the kitchen".

Also ensconced at Mabel's estate was the artist Georgia O'Keefe, who was busy capturing the southwest in evocative paintings that would become synonymous with the region for decades. Ella watched an eclectic mix of folk come to Mabel's desert retreat, either as houseguests or drop-in visitors: "writers from New York passing through, Indian chiefs, stately and taciturn; householders from Taos and Santa Fe". Guests also included an English woman, Dorothy Brett, who had been part of Virginia Woolf's Bloomsbury group and was lured to New Mexico by D.H. Lawrence. She soon became known for her sensitive capture of local Indian life on canvas. Lesser known but colorful, Spud Johnson, a journalist-wanderer who published a satirical magazine called *Laughing Horse*, set up his printing press in the desert. Many of these artist refugees from everywhere would ultimately settle in the area.

Ella came to know the flamboyant, often difficult, Mabel Luhan enough to poke some fun at her, through the lens of reincarnation: "Of course, Mabel was once a Roman senator; I see her quite well, with that ruthlessness, that invincible swing of her toga!" Mabel would nonchalantly banish someone from her home

– usually Dorothy Brett – out of some mysterious dislike, and then welcome the same person back with effusive attention. Later, when Ella thought back to her New Mexico experiences, it was easy to picture Mabel lying abed in the morning, propped up with pillows, writing her memoirs. Then she would sally forth on a snow-white horse to ride in the desert, and sometimes she deigned to ask Ella along, loaning her, cunningly, a quite spirited mount. Ella was up to the challenge, comfortable on a horse from her years of riding as a child.

Ella also stayed at the house Dorothy Brett ultimately constructed for herself, called The Tower Beyond Tragedy, built near the D.H. Lawrence ranch. Lawrence was long dead, but his wife Frieda returned often to visit Dorothy and live among the surprising tall pines that flourished in mountains above the desert. Ella stayed in Dorothy's guesthouse, but sometimes at night Ella would leave the comfort of her cottage to camp out next to a stream and listen to the sounds of the night – a flock of wild turkeys rustling nearby, coyotes sending signals to one another in the darkness.

Ella's New Mexico memories included a vignette about the artist Georgia O'Keefe at a horse race in Taos that carried reminders of Ella's old Dublin organisation, the *Fine*, and its Nazi-like salutes, many years before most people had ever heard of Hitler. As the crowd cheered on their favorite racers – Taos Indian, Mexican and Caucasian – Ella noted that the white spectators were few and "showed a marvelous lack of enthusiasm". She wondered whether she and other Anglos in attendance should not "support the supremacy of the white race more efficiently", just as a car pulled into the race site bearing O'Keefe. Ella described her as "slim, elegant, faultlessly gowned, dowered with that poise and elegance which have made the white race revered for centuries". With Georgia's presence, Ella felt that the dearth of white fans had been addressed and then turned her attention back to the races.

The incident, noted in Ella's autobiography, may have been written in a lightly ironic and conversational tone; still, the words created some ambiguity when set in uncompromising type without the benefit of voice and inflection. Or did Ella's aristocratic background actually reflect her sense of a superior white race?

One particular New Mexico association revisited Ella's Dublin years and held political connotations as well as artistic ones. In Taos, Ella met Ernie O'Malley, a Dubliner who had been a prominent member of the Irish Republican Army during Ireland's freedom struggle. O'Malley, who became known as the "IRA Intellectual" for his mixed personality of writer, thinker and fighter, also came to America and felt the lure of Taos. He eventually went back to Ireland, but while in New Mexico he sought out Ella's help on a book he was writing about his experiences in the IRA and the heady years of passion and conflict they shared in Ireland. Although Ella would later be given at least partial credit for co-writing O'Malley's subsequent book, *Army without Banners*, her involvement was much more limited and largely confined to such advice as: "I think that a big book like your book on Ireland takes *time*. One must stop now and then and do something else to let the work of the book mature in one's mind."

Their paths had never crossed in wartime Dublin, but Ella felt a bond with Ernie O'Malley. Both had supported the civil war rather than accommodate the Free State government backed by Britain. Both had a deep affection and respect for Ireland's west, seeing it as the wellspring of a noble Irish culture. O'Malley had grown up near the west's Achill Island, where Ella had spent time. Both pursued their fascination with the "west" into America's most rugged reaches. Surely, those similarities must have been enhanced by the enjoyment of each seeing a countryman in America, of connecting with someone who spoke the cultural language of Ireland.

Ella had vowed to stay in New Mexico "as long as it lets me". But her life was always closely linked to California, where she taught and where most of her friends resided. Ella was destined for an entirely new chapter of her life and yet another like-minded community. Even before her lectureship at Berkeley ended, Ella had thought often of her time spent in the San Luis Obispo area and the quiet country lanes of Halcyon where she had lived briefly shortly after coming to California. In her late 60s she returned to her old haunts south of San Luis Obispo, to the coastal town of Oceano, where she would write more books, meet the mystical beach dwellers of the area and live out her life.

Chapter 7

Drifters, Dreamers and Mystical Dunes

"I saw the seven [space] ships ... always look up because that's where things happen."

Amid the dunes that snaked the beach below the tiny town of Oceano, California, Ella met two hermits: George the Evangelist and Arthur the Navigator. George, with his wild white beard and the Christian sermons that had earned him his title, usually roamed the beach nude. In Ella's presence he was "clad in a suntan and a loin cloth". Arthur, a Dubliner like Ella, was also an Irish westward wanderer, although he had meandered toward the Americas as a seaman and served in the Ecuadorian navy – hence the name "Navigator". On the beach, he spun tales of the sea and carved driftwood into fanciful shapes. George and Arthur were among an eclectic group of dreamers and drifters known as Dunites, so named because they lived in crude little shacks among the coves of the beach and *saw the dunes as infused with mystical spirits and splendid powers.*

Ella naturally gravitated toward such a community and first ventured onto the beach to visit with the most famous Dunes dweller of them all: Gavin Arthur, astrologer and grandson of the American president Chester Alan Arthur. She had met Gavin when he visited his ancestral Ireland at the height of its bitter independence struggle in the early 1920s. So impassioned was he about Ireland's cause and culture, he rejected the life of politics and power of his grandfather, and abandoned the prestigious name of Chester Alan III in favour of Gavin, the Gaelic form of "Alan". During that visit, he threw himself into the struggle for independence, and, as Ella remembered him in Dublin, was ready to shoulder a weapon and march into battle. Ella tried to caution him that the fight was long and arduous, and that – as a Yankee – he would tire of the commitment.

He did return to his own country, and when Ella encountered him again in Oceano, Gavin was dreaming grand dreams of a utopian Dunite society, a peaceful, cooperative community in the dunes. He wholeheartedly embraced life on the beach, digging for clams, catching the odd fish now and then, and cooking over an open fire. No matter that he had a comfortable Victorian house elsewhere and continued, effortlessly, to inherit ample sums of money. Over the years, he had also collected four wives and various gay partners. Because of his privileged background, he had had a classical education and could converse comfortably on a wide range of subjects. Under the Oceano stars, Ella sat with him and other Dunites; they talked of cosmic matters and lost civilizations. Ella told her magical stories from Western Ireland, and, around the fire, they all drank Gavin's fine Irish whiskey late into the night.

A s Ella later recalled those evenings, "we did not succeed in solving one cosmic problem". At that time, in 1932, Ella briefly contemplated Gavin's simple life of a hermit by the sea, but she contented herself with dropping into his cove for the heady conversations that leaped from topic to topic. This was indeed the kind of group that Ella had sought ever since leaving similar, mystically-inclined friends in Dublin. For roughly thirty years, the Dunite community thrived in rustic, lean-to cabins on the Oceano beach, Gavin's among them.

The tradition of the Dunites on the Oceano coast actually went back to World War I days, when pacifists and idealists began to seek refuge in the dunes, away from what they perceived as a military madness engulfing the world. When the next global conflagration came, in the form of World War II, some returning veterans sought out the dunes as a cheap place to live within a compatible community. Over decades, many adventurers (mostly men) came to escape what they saw as a stifling corporate culture in America. They found the challenge of survival in the dunes satisfying – living on (or selling) clams, buying as little commercial food as possible, and building their rough shelters from willows, reeds, tules, sometimes bringing in redwood. They also chose carefully the particular coves that would be their home, looking for just the right energy and cosmic vibrations. According to local historian Norm Hammond, Ella understood the Dunites' search for the perfect coves; she could feel "the rhythm of the dunes and the vibrations of the individual coves."

Largely because of Gavin Arthur, the Dunites gained some modest fame far beyond their coves. For several months in 1934, Gavin published a periodical called the *Dunite Forum,* actually sold on newsstands, which featured articles on the flaws of capitalism and poems extolling the dunes.

Early on in their friendship, both Ella and Gavin realized that they had known each other in previous lives. As Gavin recalled it, he had been a Roman soldier who drifted ashore in Ireland, where he was captured and then turned over to Ella Young, who was the Priestess of the Temple, or the *Mórrigu,* meaning the "Great Queen" in Gaelic. He managed to escape Ella's clutches and was rescued by a fisherman on the coast of Ireland who transported him to a passing Roman Galley. Such experiences surprised neither of them; both reported their reincarnation experiences nonchalantly, and in addition to previous lives in her native Ireland, Ella recalled other returns in Egypt and Italy. Gavin and Ella remained close friends until Ella's death in the 1950s.

Ella introduced his Dunite community to the "Festival of the Four Jewels," patterned after the four ancient Celtic rituals of Ireland: St. Brighid in February, both a Christianised figure and an old Celtic goddess; the Bealtaine festival in May, in honour of the young gods who renewed the earth after winter; Lugh, the Sun God, and the legend of wedding the Sovereignty of Erin each August at harvest time; and Samhain, November first, intertwined with the Christian All-Souls Day, when people made contact with departed loved ones. In the late 1930s, Ella orchestrated the festivals among the dunes along with Gavin Arthur, reading chants and incantations appropriate to each event.

Ella shared with the Dunites their sense that the dunes comprised one of the world's great mystical power centres, and she saw a connection far beyond Oceano to another major mystical site: Mount Shasta, in Northern California, where Ella had once lit a ceremonial fire honouring the spirits within the mountain. Ella and the Dunites were captivated by an old legend about Mount Shasta, concerning the mystical Brotherhood of the Lemurians, an ancient culture of what some adherents believed to be the lost continent of Lemuria near India. According to the story, a sacred city – a brotherhood – thrived within Shasta, inhabited by people who had escaped from the Lemurian continent. Further south, on the beach near Oceano, small groups of people who called themselves Lemurians were sighted, chanting to the waves of the Pacific. As more interest grew about the Lemurians and Mount Shasta, Ella and Gavin were instrumental in helping to recreate a festival at the foot of Shasta, similar to the Four Jewels, calling it "The Fellowship of Shasta." Rituals of the Fellowship took place at Shasta for years thereafter.[1]

But his community at Oceano occupied Gavin more intensely than did Shasta festivals; as he focused on his dream of a commune in the dunes, he set out to create something far larger and more ambitious than the rustic shacks of early Dunite days. When completed, his "Community House" served as a central Dunite meeting place and as a curiosity for visitors who began flocking there. Ella came to visit Gavin and sip Irish whiskey in the new dwelling, where a fireplace beckoned guests amid a welter of books, some devoted to Gavin's passion, astrology, and others bearing the signature and inscriptions of Gavin's grandfather, the American president.

Ella decided that the house needed a more poetic name; she bestowed on it the title: Moy Mell (*Má Mheala*, Gaelic for "pastures of honey"), and Gavin bestowed on her the title of "Godmother of Moy Mell". So taken was he with the name of "Moy

[1] From memories of an early Dunes dweller, Elwood Decker, unpublished manuscript of Oceano historian Norm Hammond.

Mell" and with Ella, Gavin wrote a poem to honour her, and gave
it the name he had always associated with her since their days in
Dublin: "Druidess".

> She sits beside the fire, bending low
> To warm her thin translucent hands,
> And tell stories of the long ago
> In strange half-mortal fairylands.
>
> A man might think, to see her sitting so,
> That she was free of time and space,
> And in this freedom she had learned to know
> The secret soul of every race.
>
> For in the illumined magic of her smile
> And in the shadows of her face
> There hovers love that knows no human guile
> And wisdom born of inward grace.

If somewhat romanticised, Gavin's words nevertheless captured the perceptions of many who knew Ella, then in her mid-
sixties and ready to settle into a quieter phase of her life. Since
coming to California in 1926, she had occasionally stayed and
written in the cottage of Irish poet John Varian, in the little hamlet
of Halcyon, near Oceano. She was attracted to this spiritual community because it was the home of the "Halcyon Temple", which
had been founded by advocates of Theosophy – a reminder for
Ella of the old Dublin circle of friends. The Halcyon Temple members practiced a form of Theosophy blended with Christianity and
Native American spirituality. While never a member of the Temple, Ella shared many of the group's beliefs.

Her permanent residency in the area came after her teaching
stint at the University of California, Berkeley, which ended in the
late 1930s. With income from seven years of teaching and reve-
nues from her books, Ella bought a hilly, sandy acre of land and a

cottage, which was actually "one lofty large room", in Oceano. The house surely must have reminded her of the little dwellings in Ireland's remote western reaches; a letter from a friend suggested that Ella's home "is the successor of all those Irish huts in the wilderness of the offshore islands in the Atlantic and North Sea filled with so much treasure". After decades of Dublin rooming houses, borrowed cottages in America, and a rented house in Berkeley, Ella owned her home at last; she named it "Cluan-Ard," or "high meadow" in Gaelic. She set about planting "pines, acacia and eucalypti", creating a jungle that has lasted well beyond Ella's lifetime to the present day. She filled the tiny house with her beloved Chinese art and other treasures of her lifetime.

Down the hill and not far from Cluan-Ard lay the beach and the dunes she loved, a word revered and always capitalised by Ella in her writings. Her early impressions of the dunes were recorded in her usual lyrical style:

> I think of the Dunes at my first coming when a silver mist concealed the sea and the outlying mountains, and I could only be aware of a nebulous immensity. The sand at my feet was golden-yellow, the wind had toothed it in patterns and ridges, there was neither beginning nor end to it.

Later, as she became more acquainted with the area, she saw the dunes and their environs in new detail: "a day it was of light that played with shadow, foam-patterned, cleft with bird-wings, whitened with wave-crests hurrying to lose themselves in the shallows: life and movement everywhere, rhythmic and tireless."

At Cluan-Ard, the great stone fireplace soon became a magnet for visitors, including Dunites, who were lured there by her Irish stories, into-the-night hours of wide-ranging conversation, and also her cognac. Ella's ever-present cat was always close by; cats usually slithered in and out of the residence wherever she lived.

For all her interior, creative life and her steady output of books, she was essentially a social creature who kept up extensive contacts with friends in the local community and around the country, and she clearly enjoyed basking in the aura of her role as California's Irish Druidess. One guest sometimes brought her grandchildren, to gather around Ella and hear her tell lively Irish stories.

One alumnus of the dunes, the late Dixon Porter, appeared at Ella's cottage one day, eager to hear Celtic tales straight from the "Druidess". As a teenager, Dixon had lived in the dunes with his mother, ran away at 15, faked his age to join the Marine Corps, and discovered the brutal reality of warfare at Iwo Jima. After the war, he roamed the country and hopped freight trains; during these ramblings, he heard tales about a mystical woman on the coast of California, a writer and poet who interpreted the old Celtic tales. Surely, she knew all about the most famous of all Celtic heroes, the mighty Cú Chulainn, in whom Dixon had a special interest.

So he headed for California, straight to Ella's doorstep, to a tiny house that seemed to him "transported from one of the fairy tales of the Brothers Grimm". Ella swept him into the cottage for a chat in front of the fireplace. She asked if he knew the Gaelic language, and when he confessed he did not, Ella replied: "Dear boy, I'll teach you some time, it's not much harder than Greek, you know." As Dixon later looked back on the visit, "the next 18 hours or so [were] a pleasant blur in my memory. Our conversation continued through supper [finger sandwiches and beef tea] and on into the night. Soon after sunrise, I left." He came away from that visit, and many more to come, impressed by Ella's conversational sweep through Chinese art, the Russian Revolution, the Italian Renaissance and any other topic that floated by.

When the conversation turned to Dixon's World War II experiences, she may well have thought back to the chaos and bloodshed in Dublin during the 1920s, even though that conflict was not a widespread slaughter among nations. Years after World War II, memories of the deadly bombings in Japanese cities were still fresh in many people's minds, certainly in Ella's, and she confessed to Dixon her worries about nuclear proliferation, convinced that the atom bomb had unleashed frightening new dimensions of warfare. But she was also concerned with issues closer to home: the redwoods, the condor, and grey whales. Dixon marvelled at her far-sightedness long before Californians ever thought about preserving the environment, but he also came to know that this passion was grounded in Nature worship, as well as environmental politics. He remembered: "We talked about everything! Time, to Ella, was a commodity to be squandered on good talk with interesting people."

A local woman named Jane Thompson admitted that upon their first meeting, she did not particularly like this ethereal, old woman who apparently lived in some other world. Gradually they became good friends; Jane read some of Ella's books and later became the executor of Ella's estate. She came to appreciate Ella's keen eye and insights, such as when Ella would insist that the two walk outside to see something beautiful in the garden: "... some little bloom on a tree or a bush. All the little things that some of us would pass over were a great joy to her." Most fascinating to Jane were the occasions when Ella "talked to her water lilies and the fish in the pond".

It was in this same garden that a spaceship appeared one day. Ella told friends, Jane among them, of a tiny spaceship, "about the size of a thimble", that had landed at Cluan-Ard, and of course, she had conversed with its friendly inhabitants. Perhaps this was part of the UFO ("flying saucers") craze across America; some of Ella's friends in Oceano reported seeing what they called spaceships. The postmistress claimed to have seen seven; Ella confirmed that citing in the sky: "Yes, I know, I saw the seven ships." She kept a record of all her spaceship sightings and communications. She once told another friend: "You should always look up because that's where things happen."

As Jane collected Ella stories, she marvelled at her friend's lack of boundaries between the physical earth and other worlds: "To Ella Young the material world was no more real than the spirit world ... the veil between them for her was very thin." Jane also observed that Ella "was never lonely. She was never without happiness." This thought seemed to echo Maud Gonne's words in Dublin, more than thirty years before, as she lamented Ella's emigration to America: "She was always extraordinarily happy." At Cluan-Ard, this happiness commonly sprang from sessions around the fireplace, and often Ella invited Jane in for a sip of tea or brandy and to listen to recitations of poetry – sometimes Ella's own, sometimes from other Irish poets. Ella also shared her Celtic mythology stories with Jane and told her that these were myths that were instructive, that represented such qualities as good and evil – just as the Bible did. Far from being musty, irrelevant tales from a hoary ancient past, Ella believed that the tales had meaning for modern people.

Sometimes Ella visited Jane's nearby home and the eucalyptus grove in back of her house. There, Ella liked to stroll and converse with elves who, she said, appeared and walked along with her, creatures "two or three feet high", as she described them. Jane envied these conversations; she herself sat in the grove occasionally and tried to see Ella's elves, but "I never saw any".

Ella's readings and strolls with the fairies came only when she wasn't busy writing at her desk. Jane recalled: "... when she was writing she simply locked up her house and you couldn't get in, she wouldn't come to the door, and you could hammer all you wanted." Ella wrote as the mood dictated, Jane remembered: "...

sometimes in the afternoon, sometimes in the middle of the night, sometimes in the morning." All around her, the floor was ankle deep in papers and letters, a seemingly orderless mass, but one that Ella understood. She also understood her creative rhythms and noted that: "Sometimes, when I feel in a good mood I work through all the hours of the day," pausing occasionally for an "orange and a few biscuits". Until her death in 1956, the Oceano years were productive; she completed two Celtic mythology books – her best-known one, *The Tangle-Coated Horse,* and her last, *The Unicorn with the Silver Shoes* – plus her autobiography and several volumes of poetry.

Of all the people in Ella's later life, none observed Ella's literary and mystical activity more closely than Gudrun Grell, a Danish woman who had come to the United States with her American husband, John, and eventually found herself in Oceano with fields full of strawberries to tend. Gudrun met her on the occasion of Ella's eightieth birthday at Hill House, the elegant Arthur home.

Gudrun remembered that Ella made a grand entrance with Gavin Arthur: a wispy, silken veil over her head, a black velvet coat and a line-up of Celtic rings on her fingers, each with its own intricate design. Gudrun noted: "She was a beautiful old lady ... with white hair down to her shoulders ... oh, they [her eyes] were so blue.... She liked to go out, and she liked to be celebrated.... She never shook hands, but at a distance lifted and extended her hands in greeting." Gudrun remembered Ella's advice on matters of fashion: "Always dress up when people come [to visit]" and "Never let anyone take your picture unless you're dressed up."

As Gudrun came to know Ella better and drove her places, she became aware of the eclectic items in Ella's wardrobe: profuse colours, soft furs, flowing sleeves, capes, fluttering scarves, exotic Indian and Mexican slippers and shoes. In California, a place long identified with the eccentric and the maverick, Ella probably felt she could express her flair for the dramatic – whether in clothes or mystical beliefs. To Ella, California probably seemed accepting of flowing scarves and colourful Indian slippers – in contrast to the Irish experience on the East Coast, where fashion and ideas tended to be more conservative.

Ella became something of a mother figure to Gudrun, or perhaps a Celtic goddess, because Gudrun perceived an otherworldly aura about this apparently frail woman with the piercing eyes that seemed to penetrate realms far beyond the ordinary. On one occasion, when Ella accompanied her on her rounds of delivering strawberries to customers, Gudrun became depressed to the point of tears about a problem with rude buyers along her route. Ella did not say anything, Gudrun remembered, but simply held the younger woman's hands until she was calmer. She seldom talked when they were in the car together, but Gudrun always recalled the connection she felt with Ella at that moment – perhaps as mother and daughter or as immigrants experiencing America.

If Gudrun admired Ella for her mystical powers, their regard for each other was mutual. Gudrun's husband John once complained to Ella that his wife was working too hard in the strawberry fields from morning till night. Ella replied: "Well, you see, she is a genius and it doesn't matter what a genius does, it has to be perfect. When she gets started doing something with a field, that's going to be a very perfect field. It's going to be something unusual and you can't do anything about it. You can't hold her."

Gudrun often drove her out to the dunes, where Ella could commune with her spirits. On those occasions, Ella must have thought about her early years in Oceano, about drinking Gavin's Irish whiskey around the Dunites' campfire and the conversations on cosmic matters that burned as hotly as the flames.

On one of her outings with Gudrun, when the two were ready to return home, the car stalled, and nothing Gudrun tried would budge it. Ella became very quiet, almost in a trance, but after a few minutes, she stirred. She had apparently been in touch with the spirits, appealing to them to cast some magic on the car, and as Gudrun remembered it, the car started. Well into her own eighties, in interviews, Gudrun told that story very matter-of-factly. She also remembered that after the lengthy sputtering and gasping of the car, Ella had been somewhat apologetic, saying: "Sorry it took me so long." As Ella grew older and her frail body became all the more frail, their roles were reversed; Gudrun became the caretaker, the one who often dropped by to see if Ella was all right.

From Ella, Gudrun learned to appreciate the "Gilpin" of old Dublin days – the mischievous little creature who was responsible for lost items about the house, an invisible, but ever-present being, who could be blamed for missing keys, coats, kitchen knives. Ella, of course, was able to converse with the Gilpin, to make him retrieve and replace an item that had caused the stress of futile searches.

For all of her warm memories about Ella, Gudrun also found mild fault with her friend. Ella could be difficult: "She could be demanding, and she saw herself as important." Wherever she went, to Gavin Arthur's Victorian home or to a restaurant, she tended to place herself in the spotlight and at the centre of attention. Others as well as Gudrun noted that Ella could be hardheaded and unyielding, a woman who ruthlessly pursued a bargain. When she sold possessions, she insisted on exorbitant prices, but when anyone admired a particular piece of art in her collection, she would easily give it away. Gudrun recalled a trip they took to Santa Barbara, where Ella went into an antique store while Gudrun waited in the car. Shortly after, Ella came out triumphantly displaying a vase she had just purchased; she was obviously proud of the shrewd bargain she had made with the antique dealer, noting: "He didn't really know the value of it." Ella liked to surround herself with beautiful – and valuable – possessions.

Growing up, she had enjoyed the trappings of the Protestant upper class, and for all her 1920s rebel days and her proclamations about the rights of downtrodden Irishmen to control their own land, Ella was essentially an aristocrat. Her old academic colleague from Berkeley, William Wittingham Lyman, had noted this characteristic in Ella, this innate sense that "the elite should lead, and the common man should follow".

Beyond Ella's aristocratic leanings and beyond her narcissistic instinct for attention, Gudrun remembered another, much more disturbing aspect of Ella's personality. During and shortly after World War II, the very name "Hitler" still brought up feelings of anger and revulsion among most Americans. Yet, Gudrun recalled Ella's strange fascination with Hitler, which Gudrun could only explain by noting that Ella "admired people who had achieved power, like Hitler". Ella also told Gudrun that Hitler had always encouraged the arts in his country, an appealing notion to the creative spirit in Ella, because – as she told Gudrun – "artists are a little closer to God". To Ella, that aspect of Hitler – true or not – loomed more important than politics and war. Perhaps she knew that he had first aspired to be a visual artist as a young man and became embittered by his rejection from the Viennese Academy of Fine Art.

She never spoke ill of Hitler and among her mementos – collected after her death – was his special horoscope (perhaps created by Gavin Arthur), noting the rhythms of his life and his connection with the number 16. There was a significant pattern when that number was multiplied, moving from his visit to Vienna at age 16, to his rise to power in Germany at age 32, and, as Ella put it to "his increasing power as orator and leader", a speaker who could mesmerise his audiences and move them to follow him blindly in pur-

suit of Aryan supremacy. A further link to the magic 16 was his sui-
cide death at 48, as the Allied Forces closed in on him.

Many years before, while still in Dublin, Ella had spoken of the
number 16 as a significant symbol in the early days of Ireland's
War of Independence. Shortly after the Easter Rising and the an-
nouncement of the execution of its key figures, Ella noted: "It cannot have been a mere coincidence that the Rising took place in the
year 1916, and that exactly sixteen men were executed, nor can it
be merely by chance that the surrender [of the rebels] was made
from the house, number 16 in Moore Street."

Ella was always drawn to such connections, and perhaps she
easily extended that idea of "16" to Hitler. Perhaps she could separate her fascination with him from a moral outrage about the
atrocities for which he was responsible. It would have been out of
character for her to approve of his manic drive to dominate the
world. But it is plausible that her fond feelings about Germany,
going back to Ireland's colonial domination, coloured her perceptions of Hitler. Germany, never too fond of England, was a major
source of weaponry for Irish rebels during the years leading up to
the War of Independence; Ella's fellow rebel, Roger Casement, had
attempted to smuggle German arms onto Ireland's West Coast. His
mission was thwarted and he was among the 16 rebels executed.
Many Irishmen maintained an affinity for Germany that lingered
for decades after the Irish struggle for independence had ended.

For many of the Irish, and even for those who had emigrated to
America, it seemed natural to align with countries that opposed
England. Ella may also have tied Hitler to the mystical group she
had founded in Dublin so many years before: the *Fine*, a group
that aspired to unity in all its aspects, Irish, spiritual, other-
worldly. Its members greeted one another with a salute that was
uncomfortably like the Nazi salute of World War II.

One former dunes resident, one of the few children there, stressed that Ella Young would never have condoned Germany's extermination of millions of its citizens, no matter what connections Ireland and Germany once had. Also named Ella, she worked while a teenager for Ella Young in the house and garden at Cluan-Ard. A particularly vivid memory from those days centred on the teenager's mother, Marion Thorp, who suffered from severe mental illness and had disturbed Oceano calm with loud rants against Hitler during the lead-up to World War II. This incurred a warning from the local sheriff that he would have to take her into custody if she didn't cease such ravings. The young Ella reported the incident to Ella Young, who – at that moment – was standing in her lily pond, with her skirts gathered up around her legs, presumably engaged in cleaning and weeding out the water with her toes. Ella paused briefly in her squishing to comment that Marion was undoubtedly "much saner than the sheriff".

Ella Thorp (now Ella Ellis), who came to live in the dunes at age four, had first seen the older Ella when the latter visited Gavin Arthur and other Dunites. The little girl often tagged along when Ella Young went on long walks along the beach with Gavin Arthur, or sometimes with the photographer Edward Weston. The child took for granted this daily swirl of various artists and writers in the dunes, including one named John Steinbeck, who once came to the writers' critique session with a manuscript entitled *Tortilla Flats*. Young Ella's father, William Dunham Thorp, had drifted into the dunes after Depression setbacks, accepting an offer from Gavin Arthur to edit the Dunite publication, the *Forum*. His little daughter moved easily into an unconventional childhood: swimming daily in the Pacific Ocean, digging for clams and eating quantities of clam chowder.

When she started school and stayed with an Oceano family during the week (always returning to the dunes on weekends), she became more aware of the older Ella, who lived just across the street. The young girl knew her as the strange woman who seemed to attract all the stray or disabled cats in the neighbourhood, and who gave them dignified burials when they died. As a teenager, the girl washed dishes and tidied up at Cluan-Ard, working amid a profusion of books, statues, vases, wall hangings and other momentos that filled the tiny cottage. But often she was invited to let the work go and sit with Ella Young near the fireplace, to hear her read a passage from one of her manuscripts or a poem.

Ella Young clearly enjoyed the company of others, of all ages, especially as she grew older and more solitary. Gudrun and other friends in Ella's later life never dwelled on her view of Hitler, or on any other shortcomings of a woman in whom they perceived so many appealing qualities.

One particular visitor at Cluan-Ard over the years, Malcolm Small, had attended Ella's lectures at UC Berkeley in the 1930s and had always regarded Ella as a figure to be admired and revered. As a student at Berkeley, Malcolm seldom missed a lecture of Ella's, even though her Celtic stories did not earn him any college credit. His family background was Scottish, not Irish, but he saw the connections between the two cultures, and recalled that Ella's ancestors in Northern Ireland had come from Scotland. Malcolm remembered that, as a shy young man, he had finally summoned up the courage to speak to Ella after one of her lectures. He was astonished when she invited him to her Berkeley home to join a group that often gathered for late night conversation.

Thus began a long friendship, and after he left Berkeley and settled into his own career as a teacher in Los Angeles, he often visited Ella in Oceano, staying in a trailer she kept on her property. When he drove her places, to a grove of trees, or to the beach, or any place that seemed spiritual, a particular, physical stance of Ella's, to Malcolm, best showed her mystical nature: "... she would stand in a magic spot and feel vibrations with the earth." Other memories of Malcolm's involved more leisurely, earthbound activity, such as cooking steaks over a homemade pit outside Ella's house, going out for Chinese dinner, or taking in a movie starring Greta Garbo. Ella greatly admired Garbo, and Malcolm imagined that the two, both dramatic and theatrical, "would get along very well together".

On most of her outings with Malcolm, they would finish the day with Ella's ritual visit to the ocean, where she sat, in silence, contemplating the waves. She believed that sunrises and sunsets were more infused with magic than other parts of the day or night, more connected to creation, whether in nature or among artists. At this time in her life, as death approached, Ella was undoubtedly experiencing more than her usual communion with Nature. Surely, she must have marvelled, while sitting there with Malcolm at the edge of the Pacific Ocean, that her forays into the West of Ireland had once placed her at the edge of the Atlantic Ocean.

It is tempting to assume that the edge of California signalled a transition for Ella, from her westward ramblings into new mystical realms beyond physical death, and to imagine that she might return, reincarnated in another existence – perhaps as a Persian princess, or an Indian mystic. But something about looking out over the Pacific Ocean suggested an end to her cycle of reincarnation, even though she had always spoken of previous and ongoing lives. Somehow she knew that this time was different and even told a friend: "I am not coming back."

As Ella revelled in her quiet times at the ocean and in all the natural beauty of California, she surely felt far removed from the leading role the Golden State played in a modern society that seemed to have little time or use for fairies and storytelling. On outings, Ella might have noticed that a few off-road vehicles and more than a few curious people were creeping into the quiet of the dunes. Perhaps she thought back to how she marvelled at the "yellow roadster" of the Countess Markievicz on a 1925 trip to the Hill of Tara on a road shared by horse-drawn carts. Even when she saw what were probably airplanes droning over Cluan-Ard in 1953, she described them in otherworldly terms in her journal, as made "not of the usual metal, very shapely and streamlined, shaped almost like a fish", to her, a sign of some mystical presence rather than a product of American technology. An uneasiness weighed on her in this post-war burst of American success. She wrote to a friend: "Everything is lacking to us: beauty, truth, solitude, comradeship of the Nature Gods – in a word, life of body, soul and spirit. We have bartered all these for a push-button existence."

She saw the contemporary world through the eyes of a poet, an attribute that endeared her to her Berkeley friend William Lyman. He had admired Ella since first encountering her poetry while browsing in a Dublin book stall in 1909, where he purchased a slim volume of her works called *Just Poems* for a shilling. But they did not meet on that occasion. As a student at Oxford University, he had come to Dublin to get poetry inspiration from George Russell (AE), the Irish poet who had also mentored Ella in her early writing efforts.

Lyman always believed that Ella's poetry was her strongest literary gift, more so than her adaptations of Celtic literature. Later, when he finally met Ella and heard her lecture, he recalled hearing about her personal conflict regarding AE: while she had always looked up to him, as a friend and mentor, she never forgave him for supporting the 1920s Free State government and its compromise treaty that left six Northern Irish counties in British hands.

The shared passion of William Lyman and Ella Young, for all things Celtic, created a bond that lasted for thirty years. After Ella moved to Oceano and Lyman began teaching at Los Angeles City College, he frequently drove up to visit her at Cluan-Ard, to sit at the great stone fireplace and talk about whatever current subject was flitting through Ella's mind. But usually the context was literary. Lyman remembered her for the "inward fire" that he felt animated her work and her life. He was most impressed that she had written her autobiography, *Flowering Dusk,* at nearly eighty years.

That "inward fire" was a sign of strength, Lyman believed:

> She was a strong person, a strong personality, and possibly a dominant one. She was thoroughly aware of herself and what she stood for, and she never gave in, [never] gave any concession to anything but what she valued.... She had a superiority complex. She thought that everything she did and thought was of a superior order, and that gave her strength which carried her through her life and to the very end.

As the "very end" drew near and as health kept her close to the hearth, Ella became intensely aware of her immediate slice of nature at Cluan-Ard, watching the seasons and all her plantings, the trees that she had nurtured, especially the pines:

> I pretend to myself that they are not single pines, or groups of pines – they are a forest of pines! I pretend to myself, as I sit with my back propped against a tree of my own planting, that I am walking in that forest of pines: and it has no limit but the sky-curve.

In times of California drought, she welcomed a longed-for rain:

> The eucalyptus trees have withstood the drought most valiantly, but secretly they thirsted and now they are drinking with feverish tongues. In Ireland I used to hate rain – the sounds of it, the wetness of it, the steadiness with which it could obscure the sky – I welcome rain with outstretched hands in California!

In warmer times of the year, she watched:

the glint of water in [my] two ponds. They have blue water-lilies and the pearl-coloured Royal Shiroman lotus of Japan. These ponds were a birthday and Christmas gift from Gavin Arthur whose towered house is round a bend of the roadway.

Friends gifted her with darting fish for the ponds: "strange-shaped and huge-finned goldfish, silver-scaled ones, and five jet-black fish that are not like fish at all ... and gorgeous-coloured fan-tails."

More solitary now, Ella also had time to reflect back on other vignettes of California, an international St. Patrick's night in San Francisco, when the gathering included not only Irishmen in their full green regalia, but people in all manner of costume: "masked bandits, spangled Pierrots, Chinese ladies, Spanish hidalgos", and in the background, "a loud and strange burst of music ... the Irish pipes".

She also recalled her most recent trip to Mount Shasta during a May festival "when the water-meadows were pranked with iris, amethyst and purple, and little starry flowers showed themselves by the roadways". In Ella's eyes, it became the old Celtic spring festival "in honor of the Gods who came to renew the earth – the festival of youth, of adventure, of hero-deeds".

In the comfort of Cluan-Ard, Ella was content to browse through memories of a life that spanned historic periods in Ireland and artistic success in California. She noted in a letter to a friend: "I have my trees and my water lilies and friends that I prize." For all that she revelled in her Irish roots, Oceano, California was now her home, at the edge of the Pacific waters – the end of her westward wandering.

Chapter 8

Dying at the Moment
of Her Choosing

"Life, when I said I hated you, I lied."

On the morning of July 24, 1956, the young girl who cleaned Ella's home and tended to Ella's needs let herself in, as she always did. Friends remembered that much of the maid's work had actually consisted of sitting before the fireplace and chatting with Ella, while the dust collected and the dishes sat unwashed in the sink. On this particular morning, the girl found the room eerily silent – and then found Ella dead, "half in her bed, half out of it". The maid was so frightened, it was said around Oceano, that she never again set foot in the cottage at Cluan-Ard.

In her last decade, Ella experienced the shifts and transitions of a quieter, slower lifestyle. Gavin Arthur had long ago tired of beach living and resided in the comfort of his stately home near

Ella's cottage, other Dunites had moved on and sales of Ella's books – always the source of a few royalties in her later years – dwindled. Her deteriorating health kept her close to Cluan-Ard.

Systematically, from the late 1940s on, Ella began donating manuscripts and pieces of artwork to various libraries and museums, began giving away earthly possessions, surely out of an intuition of approaching death. From collections of Ella's papers preserved after her death, it is possible to discern some of her intentions to dispense with possessions. Also, thank you letters to Ella indicated that she had developed a significant reputation as a writer and storyteller around the middle of the twentieth century. A letter from the California Library Association thanked Ella for her donation of books and also for her lifelong contributions to storytelling. Acknowledgment from the Library of Congress recognised her gift of a letter from her friend and Irish activist Maud Gonne. Letters from Yale and Harvard Universities arrived, noting her donated works. A letter from the Armagh Museum in Northern Ireland, not far from Ella's birthplace, thanked her for materials probably relating to her family.

Other donations involved more personal possessions. The Santa Barbara Museum of Art recognised her donation of a Chinese silk robe and Egyptian statue, and she who had loved and collected jewelry all her life began giving it away. Toward the end, "she didn't have a jewel left in her box", a friend remembered.

Her celebrated hospitality was curtailed some, and conversations around the stone fireplace became less frequent. But she kept up an active correspondence with friends in far-flung places and she had the leisure to write more frequently in a journal. On March 17, St. Patrick's Day, 1954, she wrote about awakening suddenly and sensing that "someone was in my bedroom. I saw very vividly a girl with tangled, loose and disordered hair ... yellow, reddish and brown ... she did not look quite human." Maybe Ella sensed that the girl represented the colourful and "disordered" days of Ella's years in Dublin, a chaotic period of war and artistic discovery. Despite the passage of time, those years of heady, yet violent activity, stayed with her. In her autobiography, amid observations about California rain and fish in the ponds, she noted abruptly: "I have tried in this book to say what the Irish Rising [revolution] meant to me; yet I have perforce given only the shell, being compelled to withhold the kernel." What was she "withholding"? For Ella, the destruction in Dublin streets, the deaths of rebel friends and her passion for Ireland's cause were probably too difficult and painful to fully convey.

Correspondence in the last years of Ella's life showed that she helped out her two remaining sisters in Ireland, Elizabeth and Mary (referred to as May), by sending them shoes and other items from the United States. A letter from May in 1952 thanked Ella for sending a check: "It is a very great help indeed." The sisters appeared to be struggling economically, and Ella was viewed as the American success story.

As she aided her family and gave away possessions, only a few friends knew that she had irreversible stomach cancer; she had always been frail, and now disease began to attack her already weakened body. Bouts of bronchitis continued to plague her. When she felt the time had come, Ella orchestrated her death so that it would become a story friends would retell, that it would embody the same dramatic spirit with which she had lived her life.

In her final months, Ella talked about dying with some semblance of dignity, before her body completely lost its vibrancy and energy, and at a time of her choosing. She did not want to "suffer and live in agony", as Jane Thompson put it, and she had declined any medical treatment that might keep her alive. She had a large collection of pain pills, Jane recalled, which Ella kept in a bowl, perhaps hoarded over time from her doctor's prescriptions.

As Gudrun Grell remembered it, she looked in on Ella on 23 July 1956 on what was usually a routine visit: "I knew, and she knew, of course, that this was the last time. It was rather late, and she said goodbye to me." Gudrun instinctively felt that this good-bye was not the casual comment of departing from each other for the night; she was the only person who sensed that Ella had decided to die that night. They lingered over goodbyes:

> She told me that we [Gudrun and her husband John) had meant something to her ... and helped her to be with nature because that's where we always took her whenever we went places. We always had Ella Young along.

Gudrun remembered that when she told her husband about her intuition of Ella's imminent death, John had dismissed it, sure that Ella would live more years.

But it was indeed the time that Ella chose to leave the physical world. From the memories of friends, one can imagine that Ella spent some meditative time as night fell, as she often did, before a small shrine that she had assembled in front of a window. All her friends were aware of the objects assembled there: Chinese art pieces, Egyptian relics, Christian artifacts, all items that she had held onto, even as she gave other treasures away. She looked out on the eucalyptus trees she had planted and at the earth she worshipped. Her bowl of pills sat nearby, and so at the time she selected, she took the required dose, and probably after more meditation, made her way to bed. Ella Young, once considered by an immigration official as too frail for American citizenship, was approaching her 89th birthday.

But as the frightened young maid discovered the next day, Ella did not completely reach the comfort of her bed. Jane Thompson was summoned, and she promptly "threw the [remaining] pills away, cleaned the room up, [and] the doctor and I never said anything" when the undertaker arrived. It is unclear whether a coroner was involved, or whether any questions arose about how Ella hastened her death. Heart failure was listed as the official cause, complicated by cancer, but most people around Oceano simply knew that Ella had always been frail and that she had lived a surprisingly long and event-filled life.

For all of Ella's seemingly determined choice of death over suffering, she had obviously struggled with the decision and had misgivings about leaving a life of writing and wandering. Among the welter of items recovered after her death – writings, works in progress, unpublished scribblings and journals – one untitled, typewritten poem, probably never published, filled with sexual imagery, seemed to encompass the ambivalence she faced. In terse, straightforward language, eschewing her usual lyrical style, she wrote:

> Life, when I said I hated you, I lied.
> Although you are so false a love, still
> I bear this burning passion in my side
> To follow you, to yield up to your will.
> Although I wait you in incessant pain,
> And hold you for an hour whose ravishment
> Is but a dream of happiness, again
> Gone, lost, again desired beyond content,
> Yet, Life, I love you. And I cannot love
> Death, who is far more pitiful and tender.
> The peace he promises is not enough;
> Not for his fartherest peace would I surrender
> This ecstasy I waited for with tears,
> These nights, these sweet irrevocable years.

Ella had clearly felt tortured by her decision to die, even as she meticulously planned her exit from the world. She had given few specific instructions about her funeral service, other than expressing her desire for cremation in a redwood grove and choosing a few favourite readings. In October of that year, a few months after her death, several friends met at the site selected for the scattering of her ashes. They gathered in a canyon far from Oceano, near St. Helena in Northern California, on the property of her old friend William Lyman. Lyman described the site: "a glade carpeted with ferns among where in spring, white trillium lilies, Solomon seal, and the Star of Bethlehem show themselves. The glade lies in an arm of the creek and at one end is a clump of redwoods." Also nearby was a flowing creek and a hazel bush; the latter held sacred status in Ireland, where its nuts dropped into water and salmon ate the hazelnuts. When Ella recounted the story, she said that all who ate the salmon became wise. Ella's Festival of the Four Jewels – her tribute to the four seasonal Celtic rites of Ireland – was held on Lyman's property for many years. Altogether, it was a simple, appropriate site, and Jane Thompson recalled: "I think it would have pleased Ella."

Lyman scattered her ashes among the redwoods, the trees that Ella had always wanted to save from the logger's ax. Her will had dictated that a portion of her estate would go toward saving the redwoods; the bulk of her modest estate went to her sister Elizabeth in Ireland. Ella had also reserved a portion for Gudrun Grell, in appreciation for the care and friendship Gudrun had provided over the years. Jane read a special passage, an old Celtic prayer that Ella had requested:

> Oh Earth, Mother and Goddess, to thee we give back this body purified by fire, may the winds be comrades to it, may the rain be a benediction, may the stars look on it with kindness, may the sun evoke blossoms from this dust.

It was a reading that Ella had obviously chosen with care, to reflect her link with the earth and her worship of it as a true "Goddess," the Nature Spirit that had long ago replaced her belief in the Christian God. Ella had chosen still another tribute – to her beloved

Mount Shasta, not surprisingly – one that included these words: "Be mindful, oh Shasta of the spirit … first nourisher be mindful, may this American hillside be mindful." A Christian prayer of Ella's choice was also said at the service, an indication that she had not completely forsaken her Presbyterian roots. Lyman, pleased that he had provided the site for all these offerings, later remembered how the mourners left Ella that day: "Above her wave [redwood] branches and beside her is a hazel bush sacred to the ancient Irish. Just at hand is the voice of the creek, stern in winter and soft in summer as was the spirit of Ella Young."

Around the Oceano community, it was common knowledge that Ella's ashes had been scattered among the redwoods at William Lyman's country property in Northern California. Yet, around the same time, at the local cemetery of Santa Maria, a town near Oceano, a diagram of the burial plots indicated that Ella Young's remains resided in "Grave 7, Plot 736, 5th Section". The site is marked by a stone lying flush with the ground, inscribed with the words: "Ella Young, author and poet, December 16, 1867, Ireland, July 23, 1956." Aside from the inaccuracy of the birth date (either December 25 or 26, 1867, according to records), the two accounts of her burial might seem contradictory.

But a Santa Maria cemetery official confirmed that part of Ella's ashes do reside in her grave, and local historian Norm Hammond has noted that it was not unusual for people around Oceano to request that, upon death, their ashes be scattered in two places. Still, cremation was not common in Ella's day, and in some quarters, frowned upon. Until the 1990s, it was illegal to scatter ashes anywhere other than at sea, three miles from shore. So, clearly, the scattering of Ella's ashes at Lyman's Northern California estate was done outside the law. Perhaps Jane Thompson, her executor, chose the gravesite to give the appearance of total compliance with the three-mile rule.

No doubt, the funeral plans had always focused on the scattering of some of Ella's ashes among the natural beauties she worshipped. In any event, we can assume that Ella would not have wanted her remains to be held in a cemetery that stole space from more open areas. She believed graveyards were a desecration of that sacred Nature.

Her own piece of sacred Nature in Oceano – Cluan-Ard – seems, even today, haunted by the spirit of the woman who named it. The present owner, Peggy Weedon, chose to keep the tiny house and most of the grounds just as Ella left them in 1956. Peggy and her husband bought the property from Ella Young's estate for their own home, but they felt something of her aura and something of her personality that seemed worth saving. A portion of the land has been sold, but Peggy has held onto the area directly surrounding the cottage and to many trees and plants nurtured by Ella; the wild, tangled mass of greenery eschews the neat, orderly plots of nearby houses. Even Ella's lily pond in front has remained, although in a derelict state.

Most astonishing – and eerie – is the exterior of the cottage. At one end, a weathered sign carved with the word "Cluan-Ard" still hangs, a memento of Ella's decision to use the Gaelic name back in the 1930s, when she bought the home. At the other end, a clay likeness of her face – although not a direct mask – stares into the eyes of visitors and captures Ella's ethereal gaze. The gate leading up to the cottage is decorated with a carving of a unicorn, added well after her death and probably as a tribute to Ella's last Celtic mythology book, *The Unicorn with Silver Shoes.*

The final book of Ella's career was her autobiography, *Flowering Dusk,* and the last few pages give some sense of Ella's acknowledgement that her relentless westward journey might be ending. Published in 1945, when Ella was 78, some final passages indicated that she did not anticipate her life continuing for another ten plus years. One such passage, a memory of seeing a "lovely flight of birds in wedge formation" seemed to imagine her own flight:

> They were dazzling white of body and breast, but the wings had a bold pattern in black feathers. Knowledgeable people [had always] maintained that they were wild swans, but they bore no likeness to wild swans as I had seen them rise in Ireland from river inlets and reedy meadows: a crowded whiteness, winging heavily to the next alighting-place. These aeronauts had no thought of a speedy alighting. I am content to remember them without a name, beautiful in wedge formation, winging with such surety of purpose to a place far off. I too shall be setting forth to a place far off: a joyous and winged adventure, be it through sunshine or through storm.

Ella's countryman, the iconic James Joyce who, in *Ulysses*, wrote what many critics consider the most important novel of the twentieth century, probably did not know her, although perhaps their paths crossed going to or from the Trinity College library, or at some Dublin literary salon. Joyce would have had little understanding of Ella's obsession with Ireland's past or her journeys into the West of Ireland in pursuit of the old stories. And yet, his most famous short story, "The Dead," dwelled on themes that extended the idea of the West far beyond geographical locations. At the story's conclusion, the main character, Gabriel, reflects on the fact that he has not paid enough attention to the western part of his country, as the repository of authentic Irish culture – relatively free of British influence.

In the final paragraph of "The Dead," Gabriel says that "the time had come for him to set out on his journey westward". Traditionally, the idea of the west and of sunset has denoted death. But as a character of Joyce's creation, Gabriel comes to see the West as a place, or state of mind, of passionate, authentic living. Throughout her life, Ella Young embraced that idea, in her relentless trek westward from Dublin to the West of Ireland, to America's East Coast, to California. More importantly, her mystical vision took her into an expanded West, into worlds beyond most humans' imaginings. Whether one accepts or rejects Ella's easy connections with other-worldly spheres, it is not difficult to envy someone who has seemingly crossed over into tantalisingly mysterious realms.

Her earthly life ended in a tiny cottage in Oceano, California, as far west in America as she could travel. Ella did stress to a friend that "I am not coming back," presumably meaning that she did not foresee another reincarnation of earthly life. While it is not clear whether Ella's worship of Nature involved any sense of an afterlife, she surely imagined some existence beyond earth, as suggested in her musings about the "lovely flight of birds" over her house and her own "joyous and winged adventure".

Among her last lines in *Flowering Dusk* are words that offer a thoughtful musing for all who contemplate their own passing, even though they might share none of Ella Young's exotic visions. In a reference to a Greek mythological symbol of resurrection and immortality, Ella wrote: "At end of all, what does one have when one is old? Some wisdom perhaps; many memories, certainly; and if one is lucky, a feather shaken from the Phoenix-Bird."

This end-of-life reflection on the story of Ella's westward trek might well signal a conclusion, since this exploration of her life was not intended as a critical biography nor as a modern guide to her literary output. Today, her writings are relegated to the archives of an outdated era of Celtic literature. Still, her books – with their embodiment of a rich Irish heritage and with their mirror into Ireland's "flowering" in literature – invite the following brief view of Ella Young's literary legacy, her publishing adventures, and her own biography.

Chapter 9

Writing the Lost Legacy

"Say I was follower of the Flame,
Say that I chose the deathless Rose."

*It was drawing toward night, and the Gubbaun
Saor had not given a thought to his sleeping place. All
about him was the sky, and a country that looked as if
the People of the Gods of Dana [ancient race of gods
that inhabited Ireland in pre-Celtic times] had been
casting shoulder-stones in it since the beginning of time.
As far as the Gubbaun's eyes travelled there was stone;
grey stone, silver stones, stones with veins of crystal
and amethyst, stone that was purple to darkness;
tussocks and mounds of stones; plateaus and crags and
jutting peaks of stone; wide, endless spreading deserts
of stone. Like a jagged cloud, far off, a city climbed the
horizon.*

*The Gubbaun Saor sat down. He drew a barley cake
from his wallet, and some cresses. He ate his fill and
stretched himself to sleep.*

The pallor of dawn was in the air when a shriek tore the sleep from him. He sat up: great wings beat the sky making darkness above him, and something dropped to the earth within hand-reach. He fingered it – a bag of tools! As he touched them he knew he had the skill to use them though his hands had never hardened under a tool in his life. He slung the wallet on his shoulder and set off towards the town. – From *The Wonder Smith and His Son,* Ella Young

A brief look into Ella's writings cannot fully convey the spirit of Celtic mythology that pervaded her writing and lectures, nor capture what the tradition meant in her life. But a dip into a few of these books serves to show who Ella was, and how she saw her craft in a genre of literature too often assigned to the realm of children, dismissed as irrelevant, simplistic little tales with no cultural meaning for adults. Over the years, her tales – at least in the eyes of faithful readers and publishers – began to transcend the gap between children and adult readers, but Ella had always known that her stories reflected a culture worth exploring by people of every age.

In the foreword of one book, Ella explained that it was written "for children (and grownups)," her parentheses suggesting that adults would themselves love tales that they had perhaps heard, or heard of, in their childhoods. She characterised her readers as those "who hunger as I did for a lost inheritance", expressing her sense that the native Irish culture had been too long hidden under colonial rule. These tales had not been any major part of her own Anglo-Irish childhood; she had discovered them much later, and with regret, as an adult.

Above all, Ella's work showed the traditional Celtic impulse toward journey, movement, adventure. This characteristic is clearly evident in the story of the Gubbaun Saor, long a favorite of people Ella met in the West of Ireland. Ella adapted this legend in *The Wonder Smith and His Son,* which was published shortly after she came to America. In oral tradition over centuries, the Gubbaun Saor came to represent the village craftsman and the able man who wandered the countryside, using his skills as a builder, becoming a hero who fashioned great monuments and lifted terrible curses from villages.

When he received that bag of magic tools, dropped from the sky by crows, he set out on the road to try his gifts. Soon, he wandered into a place "where a great chief's dun was a-building." But the craftsmen at the site were squabbling among themselves about how to design the best emblem for the fortress, one that would mark it and show any evil-doers the great power of the chieftain within. Each worker wanted to garner some glory for himself in the project; all spurned the Gubbaun's offer of help and went off to rest and to continue arguing. In their absence, the Gubbaun took out his tools and fashioned an imposing "King-Cat ... more terrible than a tiger! ... bristling with fierceness", an emblem that incorporated all the ideas of the warring craftsmen. When they returned, they beheld the magnificent King-Cat, ceased their petty wrangling and begged the Gubbaun to stay and work with them.

But the Gubbaun Saor moved on and continued his wandering, as was his wont. Such legends could teach, as well as entertain, as the Gubbaun Saor showed in bringing the craftsmen together, even with their differences. In her foreword to *The Wonder Smith,* Ella noted: "It took me nearly 20 years to gather what I have in this book." She first heard about the hero of this saga on Achill Island, on the western edge of Ireland, from "an old man [shanachie] of eighty", as he guided her along the edge of dizzying cliffs that dropped "a thousand feet to the sea". Over the twenty years that Ella described, she heard versions of the Gubbaun tale at various Irish sites, and with each, her story expanded to embrace the legend in all its forms.

In his review of *The Wonder Smith and His Son*, Padraic Colum, Irish poet and longtime friend of Ella's, described his reading of it as "an odd delight – the delight of one who has come upon something that is real treasure-trove – amber beads, pieces of bronze shaped into strange patterns, animal figures in black bog-oak". He felt a sense of discovery in Ella's book, that of a reader digging into the authentic Irish tradition and finding "amber beads, pieces of bronze," as if from an archeological site. Padraic also noted that Ella's style of rendering what might have been musty legends made them highly appealing to children of the time: "I have given *The Wonder Smith and His Son* to intelligent children of ten and twelve and they have been enchanted with the stories. So it may be that the Gubbaun Saor, who is still a living character to children and grown-up people in rural parishes of Ireland [1920s] is about to become known to a wider circle." Discussing all of Ella's books on Celtic mythology, literary critics noted Ella's ability to make the old legends accessible for her generation.[1]

In the fall of 1925, as she was writing the forward to *The Wonder Smith* in New York, Ella noted: "I am revising these stories for publication in a country that is all delicate pale gold, and the ghost of pale gold, and tawny orange and bronze and amber and russet color," a reference to the trees of New England and their explosion of autumn hues. She went on to signal her goal of reaching beyond Ireland and illuminating its heritage for American readers and lis-

---

[1] Among the reviews: Padraic Colum, *Dublin Magazine*, November 1923; Annie T. Eaton, *The Horn Book*, August 1933; Padraic Colum, *The Horn Book*, May 1939.

teners: "I would wish to have for this book the good will of Ireland and America."

In 1909, some fifteen years before Ella expanded her readership to Americans, Ella published her first book, *The Coming of Lugh*, featuring a central figure in Celtic mythology – Lugh, the Sun God. In Ella's telling, Lugh was filled with light that emanated out to all around him. He set out on a long journey from the Otherworld, a site known to the Celts as a place of happiness and light, in Ella's words, "a beautiful country, shining with the colours of the dawn." Lugh resembled a Christ-like saviour figure who travelled from his paradise into a dark, unhappy Ireland ruled by an evil one-eyed tribe, the Fomorians. He appeared at the fort of the Tuatha dé Danann, the true gods of Ireland, and convinced the King Nuada that he, Lugh, possessed all the skills necessary to join the gods: that of carpenter, smith, poet, historian, and physician – among many other attributes. All of these earned him the reputation as a god of multitudinous skills. Eventually, he led the Tuatha dé Danann into battle against the Fomorians and restored Ireland to its former life of peace; his was one of the stories Ella used to inspire Irishmen of her day to fight the enemy of the early twentieth century.

This book was followed by the *Celtic Wonder Tales* in 1910, a collection of stories that roamed through many of Ireland's well-known legends, including Lugh and the Gubbaun Saor, but also into the oft-repeated story of another journey: that of the Children of Lir. In this tale, the widowed King Lir took a second wife, but, sadly, she became so jealous of Lir's four beautiful children that she transformed them into white swans and banished them from their happy home. They were sentenced to fly and swim for 300 years in one sea, then 300 years in another, and still another 300 years in a third sea. Lir, who swiftly turned his wife away from his home, went down to the water's edge and called out to his swan-children to return. But they had had a taste of life on the wing, and they told him that they had "the hearts of wild swans and we must fly in the dusk and feel the water moving under our bodies." They could not heed his plea because "in their heart was the gladness of swans when they feel the air beneath them and stretch their necks to the freedom of the sky." The words easily connect to an understanding of Ella, a woman who left her own country of legend and familiarity to "fly into the dusk", literally into the unknown – as did millions of other immigrants.

Tales told to the children of AE, Ella's old friend and mentor back in Ireland, formed the core of Ella's book, *The Unicorn with Silver Shoes* (1932), written well after Ella's reputation as a Celtic storyteller had secured her passage to America. The young wanderer in this story, the son of Balor, was Ella's own creation, rather than a tale handed down through tradition. In the book, she envisioned the son of the evil one-eyed King of the Formorians, and once she had created the character, she could never be quit of him until she disposed of him in a book. He was an unlikely hero not at all in the hero mold of Lugh or The Wonder Smith, and some critics saw him as the most human of all Ella's characters. He amused children because, as Ella put it, "he was not a model of all the seven deadly virtues". Unhappy with the idle life of a king's son, he set out to find a white horse that could traverse both land and water, ambling and bumbling through his adventures as would many humans. Along the way he took on the trade of a blacksmith and happened upon a sleeping unicorn. He fashioned shoes for this magical creature and attempted to fit them onto the unicorn, who woke up and "kicked [the Balor's son] into an apple tree". When the son tried again, the unicorn crumpled up and vanished; for the Balor's son, this was clearly not the victory of a Celtic hero and more likely Ella's acknowledgment of life's jolts and setbacks along the journey.

Returning to the hero tradition in the last and most well known of her Celtic books, Ella wrote *The Tangle-Coated Horse* (1939). This adaptation of the old story-cycle known as the Fionn Saga swept through episodes of wandering fighters led by the mighty Fionn mac Cumhaill. Perhaps the book's appeal – and the centuries-old appeal of the saga – sprang from the fact that the story moved through all of Ireland and the Gaelic regions of Scotland, giving it the sweep of journey on a grand scale. Popularly called "Finn MacCool", he was arguably the best known hero of Celtic mythology. According to the story, he was raised under the protection of a woman guardian, Bovemall, from whom he learned the ways of the forest and the skills of a warrior. He and his band of followers hired themselves out to combat evil wherever they encountered it. The title, *The Tangle-Coated Horse,* came from one particular tale of Fionn's seventeen warriors who mounted a wild, massive horse and attempted to subdue it, before it plunged all of them into the sea: "... the horse slackened speed not at all. *Splash*, he went through the wave swirls ... till horse and man and riders slipped between the sea and the sky and went over the edge of the world."

Such fanciful stories appealed to children and to many adults of Ella's day, those naturally inclined to accept the seemingly magical and absurd. Ella herself always seemed to live between fantasy and the reality of the physical, work-a-day world around her. Her years as an elementary school teacher in Dublin naturally led her into adapting the old tales for children, once she had gotten a taste of the old sagas from the West of Ireland. In her travels, she observed the language and flourishes of that region's storytellers, and she adapted them to written form.

Ella also produced several volumes of poetry over the years, although her modest fame in the 1930s and '40s came from her Celtic mythology books; a few snatches from collections written in America are relevant here. Her love of travel and the American West surfaced in her poetry, as evidenced in these lines, from a poem called "Voyage" in the 1939 collection, *Marzilan*: "Set foot on board ere she lifts and sways/with a year's sails unfurled,/for we will go adventuring over the rim of the world." Ella's poetic style began to move away from the more formal verse of her Dublin days – but her writing, even in later life, carried echoes of another age and also reflected the influence of her writing for children. In the same volume she paid tribute to Mount Shasta in Northern California, a site that reminded her of sacred places in Ireland that contained whole communities of mystical spirits. These lines convey her sense of a mountain that would outlive all wispy human endeavour, one embodied with a feminine presence:

> You are young, not out-wearied at all
> With your comrade the sun:
> We are clouds that drift and must go,
> Leaves that tremble and fall,
> Shadows that pass,
> O Mother, O Maiden, you know
> Us and the flowers in the grass.

A later volume of poetry, *Smoke of Myrrh*, published in 1950, a few years before her death, gave hints of Ella's preoccupation with the end of at least her earthly journey, as shown in these final lines, found in a typescript of the book among Ella's possessions, after her death:

> When on the stone you carve my name,
> And my hands fold for that repose,
> Say I was follower of the Flame:
> Say that I chose the deathless Rose.

Her devotion to the "Flame" went back to some of her experiences in Ireland, to her sense of the fire as the Celtic flame needed to ignite both a passion for Irish culture and as an impetus for Irish rebels of her day. She saw the "deathless Rose" as a symbol of Ireland itself, sometimes referred to in her writing as the "dark Rose", stained with the blood of its rebels, but still "the Sacred Land".

In the opening pages of *Smoke of Myrrh,* a reference to life ending and to her own childhood came together eerily on the dedication page. She had termed the volume a tribute to "Brysanthe", a name that echoed back to that particularly hateful Sunday in her parents' Presbyterian pew more than fifty years before. Her first glimpse of the little golden-haired girl who often seemed the dominant image of her childhood was perhaps an early hint of her lesbianism. Whatever its impact on Ella, the little girl's name on a dedication page some 70 years later is striking.

In the little cottage in Oceano, Ella wrote her autobiography, *Flowering Dusk: Things Remembered Accurately and Inaccurately,* in which she attempted to tell her story through the lens of a grand westward adventure. She conveyed a lifetime devoted to Celtic tradition, to the Irish independence cause, and the final chapter of her life in California. She wrote *Flowering Dusk* in her mid-seventies, seeing her life as a "dusk", a sunset, but one that was still capable of "flowering" and producing new blooms. The notion of "flowering" actually went back to Ella's view of Dublin's Irish Literary Renaissance and the Easter Rising of the rebels, a period she referred to as "the flowering dream of a people". Even in America, where she became a citizen, Ella's image of herself and her life's work were always bound up with her enduring ties to Ireland.

Ella had no problem collecting the memories of a long life, but the publication of the book was slowed down considerably by paper shortages imposed by World War II. This scarcity prompted the publisher, Longmans Green, to edit Ella's material down. Several letters to her editor, one Bertha Gunterman, showed how Ella, inclined to long, lyrical gushes of prose, reacted to the cuts and revisions. In one letter, Ella tried to take a firm stand with Miss Gunterman: "I shall be glad to consider your version, though I do not promise to abide by it." In another attempt to save her prose, she made a plea regarding the section on her visit to New Mexico, hoping there would be no cuts of the "Indian ceremonials, as I feel that I have done American culture a service in writing about them".

Still later, Ella became more alarmed: "The cuts are much more drastic that I anticipated." She hinted that she might try to find another publisher who would accept the original version, or she threatened to "shut the manuscript away, and let it hibernate until the ice age of paper shortage is a thing of the past". Finally, she made this offer: "I am willing to forgo the $500 advance . . . and donate it as a contribution to paper."

It is likely that Ella won some battles and lost some in her efforts to maintain what she saw as the integrity and completeness of her life story, which was – to her – also the story of Ireland and the western United States. The subtitle, *"Things Remembered Accurately and Inaccurately"*, gave her license to roam freely among her memories and preserve the sense of story in each recollection. Ella's autobiography selected snapshots of childhood, from the piano in the family parlour and its keys that looked like "black and white teeth", to the abandoned old castle near her home, where she visualised great battles staged from within its massive walls. Such imaginative views of the world moved with her into adulthood, into the new world of mysticism and creative energy that opened up for her in Dublin. The book then meandered through her early impressions of America and into her lasting love affair with California and the West.

The dedication page in *Flowering Dusk* showed her allegiance to her two nations with the words: "To the White Unicorn and the Tawny Lioness." Here, she reached back to her long-ago meeting with the American writer Sinclair Lewis and his observation that "Ireland is a white unicorn", linking that memory with her own image of early twentieth century America as a "tawny lioness". Thus, in her dedication, Ella celebrated the idea of place, of landscape – of a Celtic Ireland that fit the image of a beautiful, mystical creature like the unicorn, and of what she saw as rugged, wide-open sites in the American West, symbolised by the freedom and movement of the lioness.

Yet, there was another animal that Ella chose to highlight in *Flowering Dusk*, that she elevated to the status of "mascot" of the book: her cat Akbar. She persuaded her publisher to include a photo, presumably of him, the only one in the book not of Ella herself. Many casual readers probably assumed the photo was a cat, until Ella confessed – toward the end of the book – that it was actually a lynx; she justified that freedom of poetic licence by noting that Akbar "was more like a lynx than the lynx was".

As Ella finished her autobiography, Akbar "sat on a tall hassock, and never yawned through the knottiest altercation as to spelling, punctuation, and a thousand other trifles that troubled authors who, like myself, can't spell and have iron-bound notions about punctuation". Akbar was the last of a long line of cats that Ella installed in her homes, wherever she was. She believed that all cats came from a long, proud line of royal Egyptian felines. She probably knew that cats in ancient Egypt were considered sacred and often used to protect property and food. Her Akbar was definitely a warrior, a scrappy survivor of Oceano's backyard cat fights, who was finally bested by a bigger and fiercer cat.

Ella became very reflective toward the conclusion of *Flowering Dusk*, in musings that coincided with her own dwindling years. She was still writing the book even as she inserted observations about writing it, and she pondered the absurd notion of sharing experiences on paper: "The great things of my life were inner happenings – surges and fountains that renewed or inundated mind and soul. Of such events one does not write." At one point, she worried that her memoirs seemed to go "from episode to episode like those books written chapter by chapter for some magazine: to be continued in our next [issue]". Rather, she wished that her story would "meander along like a happy river that flows without interruption between green banks".

At times, she was surprised to find herself writing memoirs:

> When I was young and vigorous I had not thought of writing memoirs. I had planned to write a book on Celtic mythology. I had indeed spent about twenty-five years in preparation for it. I got no chance to write the book, and now if I got a chance I could not do it. In the limping end of life one can but shoulder a light-weight burden.

In the end, she seemed content with shaping her life story and noted upon its publication in 1945: "It is not an autobiography in the usual sense. It embodies a series of incidents, each treated in a separate chapter and forming a loose sequence." Critics agreed: a newspaper review celebrated Ella's rambling style and nonchalance about chronology, noting her "wholly unconventional collection of memories, stories, impressions". The reviewer praised her ability to mix scenes and tableaux of Ireland, of Yeats, of the creative passion of the Irish Literary Renaissance, of the rebel "Rising" of 1916. He approved of the way she could capture the essence of

Western America: "enchantment in the Pueblo country ... talk of poetry, prose and painting in Taos and Carmel.... She is always eager to talk and to listen and to see enchantment on a globe that badly needs it."[2] Beyond the critics' praise, and perhaps in a tribute more prized by Ella, a reader wrote that the book had caused her to abandon her housework: "I read a page and then make a bed, read another page and then wash a few dishes and so it goes."

Both the critic's observation of Ella's ability to see "enchantment on a globe that badly needs it" and the reader's more practical comment about the book's effect on her household duties illustrated a basic human need for connection with something beyond a life of work, beyond worldly preoccupations. That need has not diminished today.

If she were alive, Ella would surely say that many Americans have largely lost contact with the traditions of their various heritages. To Ella, mere factual history and allegiance to a government could never convey the spirit of a people. Certainly, this was a sentiment shared by one Justin McCarthy, an Irish journalist and lecturer from Cork, who travelled and spoke around the United States long before Ella did. He expressed the value of Ireland's centuries-old stories with these comments:

> The real history of most countries, probably of all countries, could be but little understood or appreciated – could indeed, hardly be proved to have its claim to authenticity – if we did not take into account the teachings of myth and legend. This is especially to be borne in mind when we are dealing with the story of Ireland.

Those comments were noted in a 1925 newspaper article shortly before Ella Young sailed into New York harbour to begin

---

[2] From Henry Hansen's review "Poetry and Patriotism", *New York World–Telegram*, June 1945.

her own American adventure and to illuminate the Irish heritage for lecture audiences and for readers of her books. Ella would surely have applauded Justin McCarthy's sentiments and seen in them her own passion for "the teaching of myth and culture".

It is impossible to know whether Ella's work in preserving Irish stories in the first half of the twentieth century left a lasting imprint on American awareness of Ireland. Over the years, academic figures at the University of California, Berkeley, did credit Ella with boosting an interest in Irish studies at that university, with her popular series of lectures in the 1930s. One professor of that day noted the "sudden flowering of interest among the undergraduates when Miss Ella Young came over from Ireland and gave her brilliant course of lectures here at the University of California a few years ago".[3] Irish Americans in general, especially in California, have always been interested in Irish literature, history and culture, always passionate and active in promoting programs and events that focus on Ireland, and Ella certainly played a role in that effort.

The more compelling reason to highlight Ella Young in a book about her life is to tell the story of an unknown storyteller, rebel, mystic, immigrant, overlooked member of the Irish Literary Renaissance and colourful personality in both Ireland and the American West. In sum, this exploration of Ella Young seeks to confirm the power of story and the human urge to push beyond limits, to move westward into new countries and new realms of the spirit.

---

[3] Comments on Ella Young's impact ranged from 1940s *Irish American Review* article, "Teaching Irish in California", by Dr Arthur Hutson, to 2005 interview with Associate Professor Dr Daniel Melia, Celtic Studies, UC Berkeley.

Sources

Ella Young's Autobiography
Flowering Dusk: Things Remembered Accurately and Inaccurately, by Ella Young, copyright 1945 by Ella Young, renewed 1973 by Jane R. Thompson. Used by permission of Random House, Inc.

Manuscript Sources
Bancroft Library, University of California, Berkeley:
    Memoirs, William Wittingham Ingham Lyman, c.1969
    W. H. Dunham, W. H. Dunham Papers, 1931
Board of the National Library of Ireland, the National Library of Ireland, Dublin:
    Joseph McGarrity Papers, 1925-1939
    M. S. and Gertrude Parry Papers, 1920
    George Roberts Papers, 1904-1926
Board of Trinity College, Dublin:
    Joseph Campbell Papers, 1920-1928
    Seamus O'Sullivan/Estella O'Solomons Collection, 1905-1925
Charles E. Young Research Library, University of California, Los Angeles:
    Special Collections: Ella Young Collection, 1916-1956.
Huntington Library, San Marino, California, C.E.S. Wood Papers 1930-31.
University College Dublin, Archives Department:
    Moss Twomey Papers, Irish Republican Memorial Project, 1924

Private Collections
James Cain collection, interviews with Ella Young's friends, 1965-2001.

Public Records
Registration District of Ballymena, Northern Ireland:
>Marriage certificate, James B. Young and Mathilda A. Russell, 1866
>Birth Certificate, Ella Young, 1867

Thoms Directory, Dublin:
>Census Records, James B.Young Household, 1901, 1911

Books
Hasia Diner, *Erin's Daughters in America*, 1983.
Mike Dixon-Kennedy, *Celtic Myth and Legend*, 1996.
Richard Ellman, *James Joyce*, 1959.
Richard English, *Ernie O'Malley, IRA Intellectual*, 1999.
R. F. Foster, *The Apprentice Mage*, 1997.
Maud Gonne, *Maud Gonne MacBride: A Servant of the Queen*, 1931.
Lady Gregory, *Selected Writings*, 1995.
Norm Hammond, *The Dunites*, 1992.
Norm Hammond, *Elwood Decker: Spirit of the Dunes*, excerpt, unpublished.
John B. Harrington, ed., *Modern Irish Drama*, 1991.
James Joyce, *Dubliners*, 1996.
Peter Kavanaugh, *The Story of the Abbey Theatre*, 1976.
Benedict Kiely, *Yeats' Ireland: An Enchanted Vision*, 1989.
Sinead McCoole, *No Ordinary Women: Irish Female Activists in the Revolutionary Years*, 2004.
Ullick O'Connor, *All the Olympians*, 1984.
George (AE) Russell, ed. *New Songs*, 1904.

Books, Historical References
All references to Irish and American West historical material came from:
>Terence Brown: *Ireland: A Social and Cultural History 1922-1985*, 1985.

Seamus Deane, ed. *The Field Day Anthology of Writing, Vol. 2* 1991.

R. F. Foster, *The Oxford Illustrated History of Ireland*, 1989.

R.F. Foster, *Modern Ireland 1600-1972*, 1989.

Charles McCarry, *The Great Southwest,* 1980.

Lois Palken Rudnick, *Mabel Dodge Luhan: New Woman, New Worlds*, 1984.

Ella Young Books Referenced

The Coming of Lugh: A Celtic Wonder Tale, 1909.

Celtic Wonder Tales, 1910, rep. 1988*.

The Wonder Smith and His Son, a Tale from the Golden Childhood of the World, 1927, rep. 1992*.

The Tangle-Coated Horse and Other Tales: Episodes from the Fionn Saga, 1929, rep.1992*.

The Unicorn with Silver Shoes, 1932, rep. 1968*.

Marzilan and Other Poems, 1938.

Flowering Dusk: Things Remembered Accurately and Inaccurately, 1945.

Smoke of Myrrh, 1950. *Reprinted by Floris Books, Edinburgh, Scotland

Articles

Padraic Colum, "Ella Young: a Druidess", *The Horn Book,* May 1939.

Anne T. Eaton, "Ella Young's Unicorns and Kyelins", *The Horn Book,* August 1933.

"Ella Young is Welcomed by Friends Here", *San Francisco Chronicle,* undated, c. 1931.

Richard Ellman, "The Backgrounds of 'The Dead'", *Modern Irish Drama,* 1991.

Elsa Gidlow, "Ella Young: Druidess", *Women Spirit,* Winter 1976.

Anne Hadden, "Off the Beaten Track with Ella Young", *The Horn Book,* May 1939.

Harry Hansen, "Poetry and Patriotism", *New York World-Telegram,* 2 June 1945.

Dr. Arthur Hutson, "Teaching Irish in California – Problems and Progress", *Irish American Review,* undated, c. 1945.

Una Jeffers, "People Are Talking" column, *The Carmel Pine Cone,* 20 December 1935.

"The Story of the Storyteller", no author, *Berkeley Gazette,* February 1981.

Eve Riehle, "The Shining World of Ella Young", *Dublin Magazine,* April/June 1958.

Ella Young, "Autobiographical Sketch of Ella Young", *The Junior Book of Authors,* 1934.

Personal Interviews

With friends of Ella Young:

Ella Thorp Ellis, 12 August 2007

Gudrun Grell, 27 July 2004

Dixon Porter, 30 August 2005

Malcolm Small, 10 April 2006

Dr Daniel Melia, Associate Professor, Celtic Studies, University of California, Berkeley, January 2005.

Peggy Weedon, owner of Ella Young's former Oceano residence, 27 July 2004.

Radio Interview

KPFA Radio, Berkeley, California:

Audiotape, interview program with Ella Young, c. 1950

Picture Credits

(In order as shown – some photographers unknown)

Cover:

Photograph of Ella Young from promotional brochure by William Feakins, New York (Box 25), Ella Young Papers (Collection 402), Department of Special Collections, Charles E. Young Research Library, UCLA.

Centre Section:

Elizabeth Young, Ella's actress sister, Peggy Weedon collection

Ella, *Celtic Wonder Tales,* by Rose McMahon

Art by Maud Gonne, *Celtic Wonder Tales*, 1988 reprint, Floris Books

Ella, cover of promotional brochure; courtesy of Charles E. Young Research Library, Special Collections, University of California, Los Angeles.

Ella's cottage, and cottage with gate, by Rose Murphy

Ella on horseback, New Mexico

Portrait of Ella Young by Ansel Adams. Collection Center for Creative Photography, University of Arizona ©The Ansel Adams Publishing Rights Trust

Art by Maud Gonne, *Celtic Wonder Tales,* 1998 reprint, Floris Books

George the Evangelist, Peggy Weedon collection

Gavin Arthur, Dr. R. W. Gerber Family Papers

Robinson and Una Jeffers, Robinson Jeffers Tor House Foundation

Sketch of Ella, by Thomas Handforth

Group in Carmel, California, Robinson Jeffers Tor House Foundation

Ella with Virginia Adams, by Ansel Adams, Collection Center for Creative Photography, University of Arizona, ©The Ansel Adams Publishing Rights Trust

Ella, probably in her 70s, Peggy Weedon collection

Ella, painting by Irish artist John O'Shea.

Index

About the Author

Rose Murphy moved from a passionate interest in several Irish women lured by the American West into her focus on Ella Young. Murphy has taught English and literature at California colleges and has published several Irish-related articles, travel pieces and editorials in American publications. She currently teaches community classes in her hometown of Sonoma, California on various aspects of Irish culture, from immigrant literature to Ireland in movies. She also stages annual performances of works by Irish playwrights. Her own Irish roots go back to Counties Cork and Kerry; she travels frequently to Ireland.